McGraw-Hill's

500
Philosophy
Questions

McGraw-Hill's

500

Philosophy

Questions

Ace Your College Exams

Micah Newman and Tim Bos

New York   Chicago   San Francisco   Lisbon   London   Madrid   Mexico City
Milan   New Delhi   San Juan   Seoul   Singapore   Sydney   Toronto

1 2 3 4 5 6 7 8 9 10 11 12 13 14 15   QFR/QFR   1 9 8 7 6 5 4 3 2

ISBN   978-0-07-178054-4
MHID   0-07-178054-8

e-ISBN 978-0-07-178055-1
e-MHID 0-07-178055-6

Library of Congress Control Number 2011944610

Series interior design by Jane Tenenbaum

McGraw-Hill products are available at special quantity discounts to use as premiums
and sales promotions or for use in corporate training programs. To contact a
representative, please e-mail us at bulksales@mcgraw-hill.com.

This book is printed on acid-free paper.

CONTENTS

Introduction   vii

Chapter 1   **Philosophy and Reasoning   1**
The Nature of Philosophy   1
Questions 1–20
Logic and Arguments   5
Questions 21–47

Chapter 2   **Ethical Theory   13**
Ethical Realism and Antirealism   13
Questions 48–63
Ethical Relativism   16
Questions 64–80
Consequentialism and Utilitarianism   19
Questions 81–95
Ethical and Psychological Egoism   22
Questions 96–111
Nonconsequentialism   26
Questions 112–130
Value Theory   29
Questions 131–150

Chapter 3   **Applied Ethics   35**
Capital Punishment   35
Questions 151–169
Animal Rights   39
Questions 170–184
Torture, Terrorism, and War   44
Questions 185–199
Poverty and Affluence   48
Questions 200–214
Euthanasia   52
Questions 215–229
Abortion   57
Questions 230–244
Bioethics   61
Questions 245–258
Affirmative Action   65
Questions 259–271

Chapter 4   **Political Philosophy** **69**

Plato and Aristotle 69
Questions 272–294
Thomas Hobbes and John Locke 74
Questions 295–309
J. S. Mill and John Rawls 78
Questions 310–325

Chapter 5   **Philosophy of Religion** **83**

God and Religious Belief 83
Questions 326–343
The Case for Theism 87
Questions 344–357
The Case Against Theism 91
Questions 358–371
Religion and Science 95
Questions 372–379

Chapter 6   **Metaphysics** **99**

The Mental and the Physical 99
Questions 380–395
Causation and Natural Laws 103
Questions 396–411
Free Will 106
Questions 412–426
Identity and Modality 110
Questions 427–441

Chapter 7   **Epistemology** **115**

The Nature of Knowledge 115
Questions 442–456
The Objects of Knowledge 119
Questions 457–472
The Limits of Knowledge 123
Questions 473–487
The Semantics of Knowledge 126
Questions 488–500

Answers **131**

INTRODUCTION

Congratulations! You've taken a big step toward achieving your best grade by purchasing *McGraw-Hill's 500 Philosophy Questions*. We are here to help you improve your grades on classroom, midterm, and final exams. These 500 questions will help you study more effectively, use your preparation time wisely, and get the final grade you want.

This book gives you 500 multiple-choice questions that cover the most essential course material. Each question has a detailed answer explanation. These questions give you valuable independent practice to supplement your regular textbook and the groundwork you are already doing in the classroom.

You might be the kind of student who needs to study extra questions a few weeks before a big exam for a final review. Or you might be the kind of student who puts off preparing until right before a midterm or final. No matter what your preparation style, you will surely benefit from reviewing these 500 questions that closely parallel the content, format, and degree of difficulty of the questions found in typical college-level exams. These questions and their answer explanations are the ideal last-minute study tool for those final days before the test.

Remember the old saying "Practice makes perfect." If you practice with all the questions and answers in this book, we are certain that you will build the skills and confidence that are needed to ace your exams. Good luck!

—*Editors of McGraw-Hill Education*

McGraw-Hill's

500
Philosophy
Questions

CHAPTER 1

Philosophy and Reasoning

The Nature of Philosophy

1. Which of the following is a philosophical question?

    (A) When did the universe begin to exist?

    (B) Who shot John F. Kennedy?

    (C) How do plants undergo photosynthesis?

    (D) What do most people mean by the term *marriage*?

    (E) Are children obligated to support their parents through old age?

2. Which of the following is a philosophical question?

    (A) How does ice form?

    (B) Is free will real or illusory?

    (C) Does matter affect the nature of space?

    (D) Why do people behave a certain way in groups?

    (E) What is the most easily preventable and widespread disease?

3. Which of the following is NOT a philosophical question?

    (A) What is the optimal minimum wage?

    (B) Who should decide whether people are fit enough to be parents?

    (C) Under what conditions could someone be said to *know* something?

    (D) Can something begin to exist at two different times?

    (E) Does time exist independently of our perception of it?

4. What makes philosophy a universally applicable discipline?

    (A) It is very easy.

    (B) It costs nothing.

    (C) It is related to many other disciplines.

    (D) It deals with issues about which anyone can ask.

    (E) It requires no education.

5. Why do philosophers pay careful attention to the principles they commit themselves to?
   (A) Because philosophers like to be as moral as possible
   (B) So that their arguments can be as plausible as possible
   (C) So that they can argue to the conclusions they want
   (D) So that they can remain consistent
   (E) To avoid having to change their minds

6. Which of the following must one do when one has made a commitment to a principle?
   (A) Have a good argument
   (B) Have a valid argument
   (C) Apply the principle wherever it is applicable
   (D) Believe in a principle that most people believe in
   (E) Further the common good

7. Which of the following is an ethical question?
   (A) Is the death penalty a just punishment?
   (B) When does an embryo's heart begin beating?
   (C) How did morality differ three generations ago?
   (D) What are the effects of life imprisonment on a person?
   (E) How much does morality differ between cultures?

8. Which of the following is an epistemological question?
   (A) How do young children learn so quickly?
   (B) How many languages is it possible to learn?
   (C) What is the best way to teach mathematics?
   (D) Why do humans want to learn so much about outer space?
   (E) What part does evidence play in establishing knowledge?

9. Which of the following is a metaphysical question?
   (A) Why do children make up imaginary friends?
   (B) Do colors exist in the world or only in our perception?
   (C) How many stars are there in the galaxy?
   (D) How many kinds of grass exist?
   (E) What makes bamboo grow so quickly?

10. Normative ethics is the subdiscipline within ethics that is concerned with _____.
(A) the nature of ethical facts
(B) the nature of moral knowledge
(C) what is most important in life
(D) requirements for right conduct in general
(E) the right approach to particular ethical issues

11. Applied ethics is the subdiscipline within ethics that is concerned with _____.
(A) the nature of ethical facts
(B) various kinds of political systems
(C) what is most important in life
(D) requirements for right conduct in general
(E) the right approach to particular ethical issues

12. Value theory is the subdiscipline within ethics that is concerned with _____.
(A) the nature of ethical facts
(B) various kinds of political systems
(C) what is most important in life
(D) requirements for right conduct in general
(E) the right approach to particular ethical issues

13. Metaethics is the subdiscipline within ethics that is concerned with _____.
(A) the nature of ethical facts
(B) various kinds of political systems
(C) what is most to be valued in life
(D) requirements for right conduct in general
(E) the right approach to particular ethical issues

14. Which of the following questions is a concern of applied ethics?
(A) Is abortion morally justifiable?
(B) Do people's definitions of happiness differ?
(C) Should acts only be justified by their outcomes?
(D) Is morality purely a subjective matter?
(E) Does the death penalty deter violent crime?

15. Which of the following questions is a concern of applied ethics?
    - (A) When does human life begin?
    - (B) Why do some people gradually change their morality?
    - (C) Should one invest money in the stock market?
    - (D) How should juveniles be punished for crimes?
    - (E) Why are there different marriage customs in different cultures?

16. Which of the following questions is best addressed by value theory?
    - (A) Why should you get out of bed in the morning?
    - (B) Which career will make the best use of your degree?
    - (C) Should two people live together before they get married?
    - (D) Should you buy a new car or a used one?
    - (E) Why do many people disagree about morality?

17. Which of the following questions is best addressed by normative ethics?
    - (A) Why are some people immoral?
    - (B) Is it ever permissible to break a promise?
    - (C) Do most people think their ethical judgments are fact-based?
    - (D) Do other animals have morality?
    - (E) Are political dictatorships ever good?

18. Which of the following questions is best addressed by normative ethics?
    - (A) Do people always think about the consequences of their actions?
    - (B) What legal obligations does a written contract place one under?
    - (C) Why was slavery once permitted?
    - (D) Why do some wealthy people resort to crime?
    - (E) Must one always do one's duty no matter what?

19. Which of the following questions is best addressed by metaethics?
    - (A) In what circumstances do moral disagreements arise?
    - (B) Is there any way, in principle, to resolve moral disagreements?
    - (C) When do children begin to understand right and wrong?
    - (D) Should people be excused for acting harmfully out of ignorance?
    - (E) Do people make moral judgments differently in different cultures?

20. Which of the following questions is best addressed by metaethics?
    - (A) How do most people go about making difficult decisions?
    - (B) Do adolescents engage in complex moral reasoning?
    - (C) Is torture ever morally permissible?
    - (D) What is the nature of moral disagreement?
    - (E) Do friendships impose special moral obligations?

Logic and Arguments

21. What is the role of logic in philosophy?

(A) To help one express oneself persuasively
(B) To find out which principles are true
(C) To express oneself in a technical manner
(D) To determine right answers to ethical dilemmas
(E) To determine, given the truth of certain statements, what else must be true

22. The logic of an argument is what dictates whether the argument _____.

(A) sounds plausible
(B) has premises that are true
(C) has a conclusion that makes sense
(D) has a conclusion that you are willing to accept
(E) has a conclusion that follows from its premises

23. In philosophy, logic refers to _____.

(A) valid structures of inference
(B) the formal expression of values
(C) what makes statements true or false
(D) what is needed to make a sound argument
(E) whether premises of an argument are based on fact

24. A conditional is a statement that _____.

(A) might be true
(B) is a valid argument
(C) depends on another statement's being true
(D) expresses a relation of consequence between statements
(E) gives valid reasons for the truth of a conclusion

25. A true conditional is a statement that _____.

(A) must be true
(B) has a true antecedent and a true consequent
(C) is such that if the consequent is true, the antecedent must also be true
(D) is such that if the antecedent is true, the consequent must also be true
(E) is such that if the antecedent is false, the consequent must also be false

26. A conditional is false just if _____.
    - (A) its antecedent is false
    - (B) its consequent is false
    - (C) its antecedent and consequent are false
    - (D) its antecedent and its consequent might be false
    - (E) it is possible for its antecedent to be true while its consequent is false

27. A true conditional is a statement for which _____.
    - (A) the antecedent is true
    - (B) the consequent is true
    - (C) the consequent follows from the antecedent
    - (D) the antecedent and consequent are both true
    - (E) a plausible argument can be made

28. A counterexample to a conditional _____.
    - (A) falsifies the conditional's antecedent
    - (B) falsifies the conditional's consequent
    - (C) disproves the consequent of the conditional
    - (D) says that its consequent may be false while the antecedent is true
    - (E) says that its consequent may be true while its antecedent is false

29. The premises of an argument correspond to _____.
    - (A) a conditional
    - (B) a true conditional
    - (C) a valid argument
    - (D) the antecedent of a conditional
    - (E) the conclusion of a conditional

30. Every argument contains _____.
    - (A) a conditional
    - (B) a true conclusion
    - (C) at least three premises
    - (D) at least one true premise
    - (E) at least one premise that is a general principle

31. An inductive argument is one in which _____.
    - (A) the conclusion is not logical
    - (B) the truth of the conclusion is shown to be probable
    - (C) the premises logically entail the conclusion
    - (D) the premises are scientific in nature
    - (E) the conclusion can be proven

32. An invalid argument is one for which _____.

    (A) the premises are false

    (B) the conclusion is false

    (C) the premises might be false but the conclusion true

    (D) the premises might be true but the conclusion false

    (E) there are no principles that are given

33. Given a true conditional statement, which of the following is a valid form of inference?

    (A) From a false antecedent to a false consequent

    (B) From a false antecedent to a true consequent

    (C) From a false consequent to a false antecedent

    (D) From a true consequent to a true antecedent

    (E) From a true antecedent to a false consequent

34. Consider the following argument:

    1. Cats have claws.

    2. Birds have beaks.

    Therefore, some horses have hooves.

This argument is _____.

    (A) invalid

    (B) invalid but sound

    (C) valid and sound

    (D) sound but invalid

    (E) valid but unsound

35. Consider the following argument:

    1. All horses have wings.

    2. Nellie is a horse.

    Therefore, Nellie has wings.

This argument is _____.

    (A) invalid

    (B) invalid but sound

    (C) valid and sound

    (D) sound but invalid

    (E) valid but unsound

36. Consider the following argument:

    1. Stars are bright.
    2. The sun is a star.
    Therefore, the sun is bright.

This argument is _____.
(A) invalid
(B) invalid but sound
(C) valid and sound
(D) sound but invalid
(E) valid but unsound

37. Consider the following argument:

    1. If fruits contain vitamins, then people do not eat fruits.
    2. People do eat fruits.
    Therefore, fruits do not contain vitamins.

This argument is _____.
(A) invalid
(B) invalid but sound
(C) valid and sound
(D) sound but invalid
(E) valid but unsound

38. Consider the following argument:

    1. If milk contained alcohol, it would be illegal for minors to drink it.
    2. It is not illegal for minors to drink milk.
    Therefore, milk does not contain alcohol.

This argument is _____.
(A) invalid
(B) invalid but sound
(C) valid and sound
(D) sound but invalid
(E) valid but unsound

39. To commit a logical fallacy is to _____.
  - (A) make an invalid inference
  - (B) make an argument with false premises
  - (C) reject the premises of a valid argument
  - (D) reject the conclusion of an argument
  - (E) draw a conclusion that is not supported by facts

40. Consider the following piece of reasoning: "If you go to school tomorrow, you'll pass your exam. You won't go to school tomorrow. Therefore, you won't pass your exam." This inference is _____.
  - (A) a valid use of *modus ponens*
  - (B) a valid use of *modus tollens*
  - (C) an instance of the fallacy of denying the antecedent
  - (D) an instance of the fallacy of affirming the consequent
  - (E) None of the above

41. Consider the following piece of reasoning: "If I crash my car, my father will buy me a new one. My father will not buy me a new one. Therefore, I won't crash my car." This inference is _____.
  - (A) a valid use of *modus ponens*
  - (B) a valid use of *modus tollens*
  - (C) an instance of the fallacy of denying the antecedent
  - (D) an instance of the fallacy of affirming the consequent
  - (E) None of the above

42. Consider the following piece of reasoning: "If we like the movie, we'll recommend it to others. We won't like the movie. Therefore, we won't recommend it to others." This inference is _____.
  - (A) a valid use of *modus ponens*
  - (B) a valid use of *modus tollens*
  - (C) an instance of the fallacy of denying the antecedent
  - (D) an instance of the fallacy of affirming the consequent
  - (E) None of the above

43. Consider the following piece of reasoning: "If they took the bus, they saved money. They saved money. Therefore, they took the bus." This inference is _____.

(A) a valid use of *modus ponens*
(B) a valid use of *modus tollens*
(C) an instance of the fallacy of denying the antecedent
(D) an instance of the fallacy of affirming the consequent
(E) None of the above

44. Consider the following piece of reasoning: "If Russia is a large country, it will rain tomorrow in Seattle. Russia is a large country. Therefore, it will rain tomorrow in Seattle." This inference is _____.

(A) a valid use of *modus ponens*
(B) a valid use of *modus tollens*
(C) an instance of the fallacy of denying the antecedent
(D) an instance of the fallacy of affirming the consequent
(E) None of the above

45. Consider the following piece of reasoning: "If you'd made a lot of money in the stock market, you'd be rich now. You are rich now. Therefore, you must have made a lot of money in the stock market." This inference is _____.

(A) a valid use of *modus ponens*
(B) a valid use of *modus tollens*
(C) an instance of the fallacy of denying the antecedent
(D) an instance of the fallacy of affirming the consequent
(E) None of the above

46. Consider the following piece of reasoning: "If seven is a prime number, then I am a gorilla. I am not a gorilla. Therefore, seven is not a prime number." This inference is _____.

(A) a valid use of *modus ponens*
(B) a valid use of *modus tollens*
(C) an instance of the fallacy of denying the antecedent
(D) an instance of the fallacy of affirming the consequent
(E) None of the above

47. Consider the following piece of reasoning: "If my flight is on time, I will make it home for dinner. My flight will be on time. Therefore, I will make it home for dinner." This inference is _____.

(A) a valid use of *modus ponens*
(B) a valid use of *modus tollens*
(C) an instance of the fallacy of denying the antecedent
(D) an instance of the fallacy of affirming the consequent
(E) None of the above

CHAPTER 2

Ethical Theory

Ethical Realism and Antirealism

48. Ethical realism is the view that _____.

    (A) moral facts exist

    (B) people think their moral judgments apply generally to everyone

    (C) we should find out as many facts as possible before making moral judgments

    (D) there are moral facts that are what they are regardless of anyone's beliefs about them

    (E) people do not use emotions in moral judgment

49. Ethical realism is consistent with the view that _____.

    (A) everyone is wrong about morality

    (B) differing moral views are all correct

    (C) moral facts are determined by choice

    (D) morality is ultimately subjective

    (E) there are no moral facts

50. Ethical realists believe that _____.

    (A) most people are objective about morality

    (B) moral truths are objective

    (C) moral truths are subjective

    (D) people determine moral truths

    (E) moral judgments are just emotional expressions

51. Which of the following does ethical realism have trouble accounting for?
    (A) People's attachment to their moral judgments
    (B) The role of truth in moral reasoning
    (C) The widespread nature of moral disagreement
    (D) The many different areas to which ethical realism applies
    (E) The role of emotions in ethics

52. The fundamental reason for accepting ethical realism is that it _____.
    (A) makes it easy to see what moral facts are
    (B) explains why there is so much moral disagreement
    (C) does not require there to be any moral truths
    (D) accounts the best for the role of emotions in morality
    (E) makes the most sense of our intuitions about moral truths

53. Ethical _____ holds that morality is *dependent* on people's judgments about it.
    (A) realism
    (B) antirealism
    (C) traditionalism
    (D) liberalism
    (E) nihilism

54. Ethical _____ holds that moral facts are *independent* of people's judgments about them.
    (A) realism
    (B) antirealism
    (C) expressivism
    (D) liberalism
    (E) nihilism

55. Which of the following does ethical antirealism have trouble accounting for?
    (A) The widespread nature of moral disagreement
    (B) The role of emotions in moral judgment
    (C) The variety of areas to which moral judgments apply
    (D) The possibility of objectively correct moral judgments
    (E) The nature of moral facts

56. Which of the following views is inconsistent with antirealism?

    (A) Relativism
    (B) Expressivism
    (C) Natural law ethics
    (D) Nihilism
    (E) Error theory

57. Which of the following views is inconsistent with realism?

    (A) Relativism
    (B) Subjectivism
    (C) Objectivism
    (D) Liberalism
    (E) Traditionalism

58. Ethical realism entails that ＿＿＿＿＿＿.

    (A) ethical disagreements can never be resolved
    (B) the moral facts are determined by sentiments
    (C) the moral facts are discoverable by reason
    (D) people can change their minds about morality
    (E) people can be objectively wrong in their morality

59. Ethical realism entails that ＿＿＿＿＿＿.

    (A) the ethical facts have always been the same
    (B) in principle everyone can agree on morality
    (C) if moral judgments are correct, they are objectively correct
    (D) people everywhere have a common ethical core
    (E) it is possible to identify all of the moral facts

60. Ethical antirealism entails that ＿＿＿＿＿＿.

    (A) there are no objective facts
    (B) ethical realism is false
    (C) everyone is wrong about morality
    (D) everyone might be wrong about morality
    (E) ethical judgments are expressions of emotion

61. Ethical antirealism entails that ＿＿＿＿＿＿.

    (A) there is widespread disagreement on morality
    (B) there are no traditional views about morality
    (C) moral facts are determined by culture
    (D) people cannot be objectively correct about morality
    (E) there are no moral facts

62. People often become ethical antirealists because _____.
    (A) they encounter a wide range of ethical diversity
    (B) they think that only their ethical views are correct
    (C) they are willing to change their moral views
    (D) morality includes many important issues
    (E) morality is ultimately subjective

63. People's ethical intuitions are often realist because _____.
    (A) there is widespread agreement on all major issues
    (B) they have moral views that seem as if they must be correct
    (C) it is easy to identify what the moral facts are
    (D) ethical views seem to be relative to culture
    (E) the subject of ethics is analogous to science

Ethical Relativism

64. Ethical relativism is the view that _____.
    (A) the right thing to do varies with the situation
    (B) there are no such things as moral facts
    (C) we should never make moral judgments
    (D) ethical facts vary according to the observer
    (E) ethical judgments are expressions of emotion

65. The primary motivation for ethical relativism is the observation that _____.
    (A) moral facts would have to be objective
    (B) there is a great deal of diversity in moral judgments
    (C) moral judgments are highly subjective
    (D) there is a need to reduce conflict
    (E) moral judgments are laden with emotion

66. Individual ethical relativism is the view that _____.
    (A) individuals may change their moral views over time
    (B) there is no way to change people's moral views
    (C) each person has his or her own valid moral standards
    (D) there is no such thing as moral disagreement
    (E) it is never permissible to morally judge other people

67. What is an ethical *norm?*
- (A) Whatever is accepted by a culture
- (B) A standard of moral right or wrong
- (C) A moral view that is held by most people
- (D) Behavior that is accepted as normal
- (E) An ethical theory

68. Cultural ethical relativism is the view that _____.
- (A) moral views may differ within a culture
- (B) ethical norms may differ among cultures
- (C) the correctness of moral norms can only be judged within a culture
- (D) cultures are too different from one another to ethically agree
- (E) everyone has the right to his or her own ethical views

69. A cultural ethical relativist is committed to the claim that _____.
- (A) any culture's moral norms could be wrong
- (B) individuals cannot be morally wrong
- (C) different cultures' moral norms must differ
- (D) morality is ultimately a matter of taste
- (E) every culture has a right to its own moral norms

70. Both individual relativism and cultural ethical relativism hold that _____.
- (A) morality is subjective
- (B) human feelings determine the possible moral judgments
- (C) there are no moral facts that apply equally to everyone
- (D) moral facts are relative to the individual making the judgment
- (E) each person's ethics are automatically correct

71. A weakness of cultural ethical relativism is that _____.
- (A) an individual is always right within his or her culture
- (B) it cannot explain why moral codes vary between cultures
- (C) it cannot adjudicate moral disagreements between individuals
- (D) nothing that a culture accepts can be condemned by another culture
- (E) it cannot explain why moral disagreements arise

72. A weakness common to individual and cultural ethical relativism is that they _____.

(A) hold that each standard is automatically correct
(B) cannot account for differences in moral standards
(C) allow people to judge those of different cultures
(D) give people the right to do whatever seems best to them
(E) encourage ethnocentrism about values

73. Which ethical theory is NOT consistent with ethical relativism?

(A) Absolutism
(B) Realism
(C) Subjectivism
(D) Antirealism
(E) Traditionalism

74. Individual ethical relativism entails that each individual is morally infallible because _____.

(A) there is no way to change anyone's mind about morality
(B) no one can judge another person's ethical norms
(C) it means that no one ever acts morally wrongly
(D) it means that there are no moral standards
(E) only cultures are morally fallible

75. Cultural ethical relativism entails that each culture is morally infallible because _____.

(A) cultural norms are historically based
(B) it means that individuals cannot be morally wrong
(C) cultural norms cannot change over time
(D) morality is ultimately subjective
(E) a culture's own ethical norms provide the only standard of judgment

76. How can cultural ethical relativism be objected to on the basis of culture?

(A) Cultures are basically the same.
(B) Cultures are too different from one another to be compared.
(C) It is hard to define culture so as to tell where there are two different cultures.
(D) One cannot object to moral norms that differ between different cultures.
(E) There are not many moral norms in common within a culture.

77. One way to argue against ethical relativism is on the basis of
_____.

   (A) ethical progress
   (B) cultural diversity
   (C) ethical subjectivity
   (D) individual differences
   (E) historical differences

78. How is ethical absolutism incompatible with ethical relativism?
   (A) Absolutism says that there is widespread agreement.
   (B) Absolutism says that there is widespread disagreement.
   (C) Absolutism says that there are moral norms that apply to everyone.
   (D) Ethical relativism says that there is diversity in moral norms.
   (E) Ethical relativism says that there are objective moral facts.

79. Psychological relativism is the view that _____.
   (A) different cultures ought to have different moral standards
   (B) people cannot in general be made to agree on morality
   (C) people believe that moral norms are relative to the observer
   (D) people most often hold to moral norms that are relative to
       the culture or individual
   (E) moral norms are relative to the observer

80. Psychological relativism entails that _____.
   (A) there will be a lot of moral disagreement between people
   (B) it is not permissible to judge moral norms of other people
   (C) most people will agree on most moral norms
   (D) moral norms are relative to culture
   (E) there are no moral norms that most people hold to

Consequentialism and Utilitarianism

81. Consequentialism is the view that _____.
   (A) every action has consequences
   (B) only moral actions have consequences
   (C) morality is a field that is consequential
   (D) actions should be judged in terms of their intent
   (E) acts are to be morally judged in terms of their consequences

82. An advantage of consequentialism is that it _____.

(A) can account for immorality simply in terms of harm
(B) gives all of the same results as common sense does
(C) encourages people to treat human beings with special respect
(D) maximizes justice for the most people
(E) focuses on human beings as moral agents

83. An action that is morally _____ is defined as supererogatory.

(A) good
(B) permissible
(C) neutral
(D) good but not required
(E) required

84. Why does consequentialism have difficulty accounting for supererogatory acts?

(A) It intrinsically values only pleasure.
(B) It cannot take account of the moral goodness of an agent.
(C) It cannot take a sense of duty into account.
(D) It is interested only in the consequences of actions.
(E) It makes everything that is morally good obligatory.

85. A weakness of consequentialism is that it _____.

(A) requires too many rules
(B) does not take into account the intention with which an action is done
(C) cannot assign moral responsibility to those who act
(D) cannot explain why many actions that we would consider wrong are wrong
(E) puts too much emphasis on the moral goodness or badness of individuals

86. Which of the following is NOT a weakness of consequentialism?

(A) It leaves the moral agent out of the picture.
(B) It cannot take considerations of justice into account.
(C) It can only consider actual, not expected, results.
(D) It cannot take other people's good into account.
(E) It cannot take account of the moral value of humans.

87. Rule consequentialism says that rules should be put in place that
_____.

(A) always have good results
(B) most people can agree upon
(C) the morally best people devise
(D) are not the same as traditional rules
(E) are such that following them consistently will give the best results

88. A disadvantage of rule consequentialism with respect to act consequentialism is that it _____.

(A) requires rule following even in cases where it does not maximize utility
(B) cannot take account of the moral value of intentions
(C) would revise most commonsense moral rules
(D) is too traditional
(E) is not impartial

89. *Utility* in ethical theory is roughly equivalent to _____.

(A) justice
(B) responsibility
(C) efficiency
(D) happiness
(E) convenience

90. In normative theory, utilitarianism is a species of _____.

(A) value theory
(B) virtue ethics
(C) consequentialism
(D) ethical egoism
(E) duty-based ethics

91. One of the advantages of utilitarianism is that it is _____.

(A) just
(B) traditional
(C) impartial
(D) undemanding
(E) consequentialist

92. Which of the following can be recognized only as instrumental in value according to utilitarianism?
    (A) Utility
    (B) Happiness
    (C) Intentions
    (D) Pleasure
    (E) Consequences

93. Which of the following acts would be considered wrong according to utilitarianism?
    (A) Making a promise
    (B) Taking the life of someone who wanted to die
    (C) Breaking a promise in order to save a life
    (D) Eating an extra sandwich instead of giving it to a hungry person
    (E) Breaking the speed limit in order to get a woman in labor to the hospital

94. Which of the following acts would be NOT ordinarily be considered wrong according to utilitarianism?
    (A) Breaking into a car to steal a radio
    (B) Stealing from the rich to bring fresh water to those who do not have it
    (C) A police officer's enforcing a law even in a case where it brings harm
    (D) Subjecting animals to testing of cosmetics products
    (E) Insulting a person to humiliate him or her

95. Which philosopher was one of the first to champion utilitarianism?
    (A) David Hume
    (B) Immanuel Kant
    (C) John Stuart Mill
    (D) J. J. C. Smart
    (E) Aristotle

Ethical and Psychological Egoism

96. Ethical egoism is the view that _____.
    (A) people will act only according to their own interests
    (B) one should act only in ways that further one's own interests
    (C) one should never further the interests of others
    (D) what is right for one person may not be right for another
    (E) each individual has unique abilities and interests

97. Which philosopher most strongly supported ethical egoism?

(A) Friedrich Nietzsche

(B) David Hume

(C) John Stuart Mill

(D) Immanuel Kant

(E) Plato

98. Ayn Rand's argument for ethical egoism is based on which of the following key premises?

(A) Traditional morality is wrong.

(B) People should have the right to do as they please.

(C) Each person should only look after his or her own interests.

(D) The ultimate value for each person is himself or herself.

(E) No one should have to act in ways contrary to his or her own interests.

99. An ethical egoist is committed to the claim that _____.

(A) it is wrong to do anything that furthers anyone else's interests

(B) everyone will have a different set of ethical views

(C) the same thing will be best for everyone

(D) there may be circumstances in which it is permissible to help others

(E) it is wrong to do anything that does not further one's own interests

100. An ethical egoist must think which of the following is wrong?

(A) Doing something that benefits another person's self-interest

(B) Giving to the hungry and thereby forgoing the means to do something of value to oneself

(C) Advancing one's self-interest at the expense of another

(D) Recognizing the fact that other people have self-interest

(E) Following a rule that someone else has made

101. Ethical egoism maintains that _____.

(A) your interests will also benefit others

(B) you should never consider the desires of other people

(C) it is always ethical to do whatever is in your own interests

(D) you should think of yourself as always doing whatever is ethical

(E) people will not follow traditional morality if they do not have to

102. One of the main reasons for believing in ethical egoism is the idea that _____.

(A) people are only interested in advancing their self-interest
(B) each person is the best person qualified to look after his or her own interests
(C) ethics is a subjective realm and each person must decide on his or her own ethical views
(D) everyone ultimately has the same ethical views
(E) everyone ultimately has the same interests

103. A major drawback to ethical egoism is that it _____.

(A) goes strongly against traditional morality
(B) does not take account of individual rights
(C) does not take account of the value of the individual
(D) cannot be supported by psychology
(E) is self-contradictory

104. Ethical egoism is a species of which normative theory?

(A) Utilitarianism
(B) Consequentialism
(C) Duty-based ethics
(D) Virtue-based ethics
(E) Natural law theory

105. Psychological egoism is the view that _____.

(A) individuals are best at advancing their own interests
(B) people should only do what is in their own interests
(C) traditional morality is too difficult for most people to follow
(D) people are only capable of advancing their own interests
(E) morality is a matter of psychology

106. Psychological egoism entails that _____.

(A) everyone is really an ethical egoist
(B) no one has any reason to help others
(C) it is useless to try to get people to do what is not in their own interests
(D) laws are only put in place to keep people from advancing their self-interest
(E) psychology is a discipline dominated by egoists

107. Psychological egoism maintains that the possible ethical theories are constrained by the fact that _____.

(A) people will only believe in the ethical theories that they want to believe in

(B) no one can really know what the correct ethical theory is

(C) there is no ethical theory that can take account of all the facts

(D) ethics properly understood falls into place as a part of psychology

(E) one cannot tell people that they should do kinds of things that they really cannot

108. How would a psychological egoist have to explain apparent cases of self-sacrifice?

(A) People do not always know what is in their own self-interest.

(B) People often do not mind giving things up for a greater good.

(C) People must somehow believe they are furthering their own self-interest even in self-sacrifice.

(D) Apparent cases of self-sacrifice are actually those in which a person fails to advance his or her own self-interest.

(E) Self-sacrifice is something that people do without thinking about it.

109. The story in Plato's *Republic* about the ring of Gyges is meant to show that _____.

(A) psychological egoism is true

(B) psychological egoism is ethical

(C) psychological egoism is unethical

(D) most people believe in psychological egoism

(E) psychological egoists should be ethical egoists

110. According to psychological egoism, people ordinarily do not do everything that would be in their own interest because they _____.

(A) do not know how

(B) are afraid of being caught

(C) do not believe in psychological egoism

(D) act in accordance with traditional morality instead

(E) have interests that overlap those of others

111. Which of the following is a drawback to psychological egoism?

(A) It is hard to reconcile with human nature.

(B) There seem to be genuine cases of altruism.

(C) It would mean that people should never give to others.

(D) It is part of an ethical theory that goes against traditional morality.

(E) There are many who would stand to gain too much if it were true.

Nonconsequentialism

112. Immanuel Kant thought the most moral actions are those that
_____.

(A) are done with the most knowledge of their consequences
(B) are done with others' interests in mind
(C) arise out of a sense of virtue
(D) result in the greatest good
(E) are done purely out of a good will

113. Which of the following is part of Kant's concept of the good will?

(A) Integrity
(B) Virtue
(C) Duty
(D) Generosity
(E) The Golden Rule

114. According to Kant's normative theory, morality is to be explained in terms
of _____.

(A) virtue
(B) consequences
(C) sentiments
(D) goodness
(E) rationality

115. Kant maintained that an action is rational only if _____.

(A) it actually achieves its goal
(B) it is done with the best intentions
(C) it would achieve its goal in an ideal situation
(D) its purpose could be accomplished if everyone acted that way
(E) there are no obstacles to achieving its goal

116. According to Kant's moral theory, the categorical imperative tells
_____.

(A) how to choose rational ends to pursue
(B) what one should always do in all circumstances
(C) what moral principles are true
(D) how to behave rationally in pursuit of one's goals
(E) how to act in accordance with virtue

117. How does a categorical imperative differ from a hypothetical imperative?
    (A) A categorical imperative contains only moral terms.
    (B) A hypothetical imperative contains no moral terms.
    (C) A categorical imperative states what should always be done.
    (D) A hypothetical imperative states what should always be done.
    (E) A categorical imperative tells how to rationally achieve certain ends.

118. Which of the following is an example of a categorical imperative?
    (A) Never cheat.
    (B) If you want to be treated charitably, you should do so to others.
    (C) If you need to rob a bank for a greater good, then it is morally acceptable.
    (D) Breaking promises is inconsistent with having a good character.
    (E) Giving to charity is a good thing to do.

119. Suppose someone says, "I am going to exercise in order to lose weight." In terms of Kant's theory of the categorical imperative, the *maxim* of this action is the _____.
    (A) goal of losing weight
    (B) chosen means of exercising
    (C) desire to exercise
    (D) knowledge of one's duty
    (E) desire to improve oneself

120. Divine command theory says that _____.
    (A) God must exist
    (B) whatever God commands is morally good
    (C) God only commands an action if it is morally good
    (D) if God did not exist, everything would be permitted
    (E) we can know God exists because of the force of moral laws

121. If divine command theory is false, then _____.
    (A) God does not exist
    (B) there can be no moral laws
    (C) humans cannot know what is morally right
    (D) moral relativism must be true
    (E) God's will does not determine what is morally right

122. In the *Euthyphro* dialogue, the central challenge that Socrates brings to Euthyphro is about whether Euthyphro _____.

(A) has a good enough case against his father

(B) might really be impious

(C) is acting piously enough

(D) knows what piety is

(E) is accusing Socrates falsely

123. In the *Euthyphro* dialogue, what is Euthyphro's answer as to what piety is?

(A) That which is just

(B) That which pious people do

(C) That which pleases the gods

(D) That which the gods command

(E) That by which we can get what we want from the gods

124. Why does Euthyphro's answer as to what piety is not satisfy Socrates?

(A) Socrates disagrees with it.

(B) It is not the answer that most people give.

(C) It is defined in terms of a certain kind of action.

(D) Socrates thinks that Euthyphro should give more examples.

(E) Socrates finds it self-contradictory.

125. The "Euthyphro dilemma" is a dilemma between _____.

(A) objective moral facts and subjective judgments

(B) God's commands being arbitrary and God having to answer to a higher authority

(C) God's commands being unknowable and God's commands being too difficult

(D) God's existence and God's nonexistence

(E) the need to define *morality* and the need to define *God*

126. Aristotle thought cultivating virtue was well suited to making good choices because _____.

(A) good is well suited to virtue

(B) good is a mean somewhere between two extremes

(C) choosing good requires a great amount of effort

(D) virtue tends to lead to good results

(E) good choices benefit everyone

127. Aristotle thought that virtuous actions can be defined in terms of _____.

    (A) whatever the most rational actions are
    (B) whatever is done with the best of intentions
    (C) what can only be learned by experience
    (D) what a virtuous person would do
    (E) what helps the most people

128. According to typical versions of virtue ethics, _____.

    (A) virtue will always bring about pleasure
    (B) virtuous actions can be done by anyone
    (C) the virtues come naturally to a good person
    (D) happiness can potentially be found by anyone
    (E) the virtues are learned by habit and experience

129. What is the "priority problem" for virtue ethics?

    (A) It explains good actions only in terms of the kind of person who would perform them.
    (B) It cannot explain how a person learns to be virtuous.
    (C) It cannot explain how the virtues aim at the good.
    (D) It puts a priority on virtues instead of morality.
    (E) It puts a priority on morality rather than bettering oneself.

130. Which of the following is a weakness common to divine command theory and virtue ethics?

    (A) It can be difficult to learn what actions are morally good.
    (B) If true, the theory may still give contradictory answers to ethical questions.
    (C) Moral goodness is defined in terms of an entity rather than an action.
    (D) They focus on moral goodness in something other than the moral agent.
    (E) They both refer to controversial standards of what is good.

Value Theory

131. Value theory is primarily about _____.

    (A) doing the right thing
    (B) things that are pursued for their own sake
    (C) the nature of moral responsibility
    (D) the value of morality
    (E) the value of theories

132. To think about the overall set of values that explains our life choices, we _____.

    (A) choose an ultimate value and then align all of our actions to it

    (B) recognize that everything we do has intrinsic value

    (C) think about what is pursued for the sake of what

    (D) likely find that nothing we do is worthwhile until we know what intrinsic values it promotes

    (E) think about what someone else would do in our place

133. An instrumental good is pursued _____.

    (A) for its own sake

    (B) for the sake of other goods

    (C) because it is the ultimate value

    (D) because it brings pleasure

    (E) in order to practice doing good

134. An intrinsic good is one that _____.

    (A) leads to some other good

    (B) is only good when it is experienced

    (C) is important for its own sake

    (D) cannot be reached by means of other things

    (E) has value independently of anything else

135. Whatever ultimate value we have in life, it must be _____.

    (A) necessary to sustain life

    (B) unrelated to anything else

    (C) something that brings an experience of well-being

    (D) the basis of an explanation for everything we do

    (E) something that we can all agree upon

136. Value theory is most analogous to _____.

    (A) music appreciation

    (B) scientific experimentation

    (C) a fundamental physical theory of the universe

    (D) explaining why a certain color is your favorite

    (E) savoring the taste of your favorite food

137. On what basis did Aristotle argue that there must be intrinsically valued goods that we pursue?

(A) If all our pursuits had only instrumental value, they would all be meaningless.

(B) It would be immoral to have no intrinsically valued goods to pursue.

(C) Everyone who lives an examined life will pursue things of intrinsic value.

(D) Things of only instrumental value are not worth our time.

(E) We can know about only intrinsically valued goods.

138. Aristotle thought that every rational person must have a _____.

(A) number of intrinsically valued goals in life

(B) single activity that he or she values the most

(C) variety of interests that make life worthwhile

(D) single ultimate value in life

(E) satisfying vocation

139. Aristotle thought that we must have *one* ultimate intrinsic value in life because he thought that if we had more than one ultimate value,

_____.

(A) our values would conflict with one another

(B) we would not be able to tell how to pursue them all

(C) we would never have time to pursue them all

(D) we could not make sense of them all together

(E) there could not be enough instrumental goals to serve all our values

140. One pursues value theory with the goal of _____.

(A) appreciating life more fully

(B) determining what morality is

(C) understanding why people have value

(D) figuring out what is most important in life

(E) determining which activities are worthwhile

141. *Eudaimonia* might best be defined as _____.

(A) happiness

(B) well-being

(C) pleasure

(D) virtue

(E) moral goodness

142. The Stoics of ancient Greece believed that _____.
- (A) happiness is compatible with the absence of pleasure
- (B) pleasure is to be avoided whenever possible
- (C) every physical pleasure ought to be pursued
- (D) being virtuous is of instrumental value
- (E) one should have no emotional responses

143. A hedonist, in philosophical usage, is one who values _____ above all else.
- (A) experiences of well-being
- (B) sensory pleasure
- (C) morality
- (D) virtue
- (E) self-betterment

144. The experience-machine thought experiment includes which of the following?
- (A) The experience of having reached all of our goals
- (B) Experiencing everything that is intrinsically good
- (C) Experiencing feelings of subjective well-being
- (D) Finding out what experiences are intrinsically valuable
- (E) Generating experiences that have value

145. The point of the experience-machine thought experiment is that _____.
- (A) nothing we experience is objectively good
- (B) experience can be gained by any means
- (C) happiness is potentially easy to reach, if only we knew how
- (D) objective values that we cannot experience are ultimately irrelevant
- (E) a subjective state of well-being cannot be the ultimate value

146. Which of the following, if true, would be a reason for thinking that hedonism is true?
- (A) Other things besides pain can harm us.
- (B) Virtue is good because it tends to bring pleasure.
- (C) We aim our activities at achieving what we value.
- (D) Other things besides pleasure are intrinsically good.
- (E) Subjective states of well-being can be produced by anything.

147. A hedonist will be committed to which of the following claims?
- (A) Objectively valuable goods are those with intrinsic value.
- (B) Objectively valuable goods will bring us the most pleasure.
- (C) Subjective states of well-being are instrumentally valuable.
- (D) Subjective states of well-being are the ultimate good.
- (E) Happiness is the ultimate value in life.

148. A hedonist will be committed to which of the following claims?
- (A) Virtue is not worth pursuing.
- (B) Objective states of well-being are to be valued the most.
- (C) Objective goods like virtue can only be given instrumental value.
- (D) Subjective states of well-being can be given instrumental value.
- (E) Subjective states of well-being are not the only things with objective value.

149. One alternative to hedonism is a view that _____ is valuable above all else.
- (A) contemplation
- (B) virtue
- (C) pleasure
- (D) happiness
- (E) experience

150. The main challenge to hedonism is the idea that _____.
- (A) hedonism requires immorality
- (B) not all pleasure leads to happiness
- (C) the pursuit of virtue does not always lead to pleasure
- (D) value theory is aimed at determining which goods are intrinsically valued
- (E) we may be harmed by something even if it does not diminish our pleasure

CHAPTER 3

Applied Ethics

Capital Punishment

151. The main motivation for the death penalty is to _____.

   (A) let justice be done on the worst crimes
   (B) give equal retribution for murderers
   (C) set an example for other criminals
   (D) decrease the overall crime rate
   (E) placate crime victims

152. Which of the following is NOT used as a basis for arguing against capital punishment?

   (A) Retributive justice does not require the death penalty.
   (B) Criminals deserve a fair hearing in court.
   (C) Equal justice cannot be used as the general basis for punishments.
   (D) The death penalty may not work as a deterrent to crime.
   (E) The death penalty would not be justified even if it were a deterrent to crime.

153. Which of the following ideas is NOT included in the justice-driven motivation for capital punishment?

   (A) There must be a deterrent to violent crime.
   (B) The punishment ought to fit the crime.
   (C) The crime of murder violates the ultimate value.
   (D) Serious crime must be recognized as such by the law.
   (E) It is the responsibility of the law to give the severest punishments when necessary.

154. The hypocrisy objection to capital punishment is based on a perceived inconsistency in _____.
   (A) exercising the death penalty when we are not morally perfect ourselves
   (B) giving equal retribution for murderers but not for other criminals
   (C) treating criminals as though they had no rights
   (D) exercising the death penalty to punish those who kill
   (E) assigning the death penalty to suspects who may be innocent

155. One flaw in the hypocrisy objection to capital punishment is that _____.
   (A) it does not give enough attention to the moral seriousness of murder
   (B) it would make it hypocritical to enforce other kinds of punishments too
   (C) the death penalty might be assessed for other reasons besides retribution
   (D) it does not take into account the possibility of proportional justice
   (E) it would let many criminals go free

156. The main problem with the objection that capital punishment may execute the innocent is that _____.
   (A) there is no way to have a perfect system of justice
   (B) there is no way to tell whether a suspect is really innocent
   (C) the objection does not tell us whether it is right to execute the guilty
   (D) it neglects the possibility that the justice system could be improved
   (E) no one wants to execute the innocent anyway

157. Which of the following is NOT a problem for the deterrence justification for capital punishment?
   (A) It is questionable whether capital punishment actually deters crime.
   (B) It is impossible to tell whether capital punishment actually deters crime.
   (C) It does not represent the primary motivation for capital punishment that most people would give.
   (D) It commits us to a principle of justice by equal retribution that cannot be generally applied.
   (E) It commits us to a principle of consequentialism that we may not subscribe to in general.

158. The justice-driven justification for capital punishment says that the death penalty is needed _____.

(A) for extracting information
(B) to redress wrongs
(C) to lower the crime rate
(D) because proportional justice demands it
(E) to serve as an example to other criminals

159. Which of the following could NOT be motivated by retributive justice?

(A) Criminals being given punishments equal to their crimes
(B) Criminals being given punishments proportional to their crimes
(C) Criminals being punished to make them better people
(D) Criminals being punished in accordance with the law
(E) Criminals being punished for the immorality of their crimes

160. The defense of the death penalty that claims it is a deterrent to crime is an invocation of _____.

(A) virtue ethics
(B) consequentialism
(C) duty-based ethics
(D) divine command theory
(E) a principle of equal justice

161. Which of the following objections to capital punishment is NOT based on a principle of justice?

(A) Capital punishment is probably not effective as a deterrent to crime.
(B) Carrying out capital punishment on those who kill is hypocritical.
(C) Capital punishment is excessive and unnecessary.
(D) Capital punishment may result in convicting the innocent.
(E) Capital punishment is disproportionally carried out on the poor.

162. What is the main problem with defending capital punishment on the basis of equal justice?

(A) Equal justice does not necessarily require the death penalty for murderers.
(B) Equal justice cannot be used to exercise retribution.
(C) It is hypocritical to kill people in order to punish murder.
(D) Capital punishment is a unique punishment reserved for the worst crimes.
(E) The principle on which it is based cannot serve as a general guideline for punishments.

163. Proportional justice requires which of the following?

(A) That the victims of crimes are satisfied with the punishment
(B) That the worst crimes are punished as severely as possible
(C) That criminals are made an example of
(D) A scale of punishments of different severities
(E) Equal retribution for all serious crimes

164. Why does proportional justice NOT require capital punishment?

(A) Proportional justice does not require retribution.
(B) Retributive justice allows only for equal retribution.
(C) The death penalty is not possible under proportional justice.
(D) Capital punishment need not be the severest punishment.
(E) Proportional justice does not require that the death penalty be the severest punishment.

165. Which of the following is NOT included in the justice-driven motivation for capital punishment?

(A) The punishment ought to fit the crime.
(B) Criminals should be made an example of.
(C) The crime of murder violates the ultimate value.
(D) Justice is the primary consideration in punishment.
(E) Capital punishment is the only way to punish the worst crimes.

166. An opponent of capital punishment need only establish that it is

_____.

(A) not necessary for justice to be served
(B) not an effective deterrent to crime
(C) harmful to society at large
(D) setting a bad example
(E) too costly

167. A system of equal justice would require that _____.

(A) criminals get what they deserve
(B) the worst crimes be punished proportionally
(C) criminals be punished with the same crimes they commit
(D) only guilty criminals be sentenced with punishments
(E) all crimes be punished equally

168. Capital punishment today is _____.
- (A) reserved for the most serious crimes
- (B) used in almost every developed country
- (C) defended by most philosophers
- (D) protected by the Constitution
- (E) used frequently

169. The most effective basis for opposing capital punishment is to argue that _____.
- (A) it is not an effective deterrent to crime
- (B) there is too much risk of executing the innocent
- (C) it is inconsistent to kill to show that murder is wrong
- (D) justice cannot generally be based on equal retribution
- (E) capital punishment is unpopular

Animal Rights

170. Which of the following best describes the relation between the terms *abolitionism* and *protectionism*?
- (A) Both terms refer to the position that humans have no moral right, and ought to have no legal right, to use animals as property.
- (B) *Abolitionism* refers to the position that humans have no moral right to use animals as property, while *protectionism* refers to the position that while humans have the right to treat animals as property, the welfare of animals ought to be protected as much as possible.
- (C) *Abolitionism* refers to the view that animal rights ought to be abolished, while *protectionism* refers to the view that animal rights ought to be protected.
- (D) The terms are interchangeable.
- (E) Both terms refer to positions that must assume a consequentialist theory of ethics.

171. What do proponents of *animal rights* typically claim?
- (A) Animals have rights that humans do not.
- (B) Animals have the right not to be treated as human property.
- (C) No animal should ever be killed for any reason.
- (D) Animals should be treated just like humans.
- (E) Animals have the right to do whatever they want.

172. What do proponents of *animal welfarism* typically claim?
  (A) Raising animals for food is always wrong.
  (B) Intentionally breeding animals for the preservation of a species is always wrong.
  (C) Treating animals like property is not always wrong.
  (D) Unnecessary cruelty to animals is not always wrong.
  (E) The welfare of animals is just as important as the welfare of humans.

173. What are the two main philosophical approaches to the issue of animal ethics?
  (A) The consequentialist approach and the deontological approach
  (B) The virtue ethics approach and the divine command theory approach
  (C) The social contract theory approach and the utilitarian approach
  (D) The feminist approach and the deontological approach
  (E) The realist approach and the antirealist approach

174. It is often argued that the contemporary *animal rights* movement began with the publication of philosopher Peter Singer's 1975 book entitled
_____.
  (A) *Of Pandas and People*
  (B) *Eating Animals*
  (C) *Animal Liberation*
  (D) *The Case for Animal Rights*
  (E) *Animal Farm*

175. *Animal rights* proponents often object to the *animal welfarism* position because it _____.
  (A) encourages the idea that animals can be treated like property
  (B) encourages the idea that animals are not property
  (C) assumes that animals feel pain
  (D) assumes that animals are better off in our care
  (E) does not take into consideration the welfare of humans

176. Some argue that it is in virtue of uniquely human capacities that human beings have moral rights that other animals do not. The best way for an *animal rights* proponent to respond to this claim is to point out that _____.

(A) severely brain-damaged infants often lack these capacities, but we still treat them as having moral rights

(B) the capacities of a species have no bearing on moral rights

(C) there are no uniquely human capacities

(D) species different from humans have unique capacities as well, but that does not mean that they have moral rights not had by other species

(E) you cannot prove that animals do not feel and reason as humans do

177. The psychological school of *behaviorism*, as championed by Watson, Skinner, and others, is often criticized for what?

(A) Encouraging the idea that animals are simply like complicated machines, whose behavior can be explained entirely mechanistically without reference to any inner states of experience (such as pain and pleasure)

(B) Focusing too much on innate patterns of behavior

(C) Promoting a view that anthropomorphizes animals

(D) Ignoring evidence that supports the idea that animals are conscious of their own existence

(E) Assuming that there is such a thing as a subjective realm of experience to be accounted for by any theory of human or animal psychology

178. *Animal welfarism* has two main opponents. Who are they?

(A) Those who believe that we should practice responsible, humane animal stewardship and those who believe that neither humans nor animals have any intrinsic rights

(B) Those who believe that animals may be treated as human property and those who believe that we should minimize animal suffering

(C) Those who believe that it is a mistake to project human traits onto animals and those who believe that animals have no intrinsic rights

(D) Those who believe that it is often necessary to cause animals to suffer and those who believe that the rights of animals should never be put before the rights of human beings

(E) Those who believe that animals do not actually experience pain or pleasure and those who believe that animals have the moral right to never be treated as human property

179. The view that while human beings have both a physical body and a nonphysical mind or soul, animals have only a physical body is widely attributed to which of the following philosophers?

(A) Plato
(B) Peter Singer
(C) David Hume
(D) Robert Nozick
(E) René Descartes

180. In response to criticisms from *animal rights* proponents, more recent proponents of *animal welfarism* have tried to argue that _____.

(A) animal rights proponents have not adequately shown that animals actually have any rights
(B) the program of animal welfarism can actually be carried out so as to eventually meet the goals of the animal rights movement in a more realistic, albeit less direct, way
(C) animal rights proponents have misunderstood or misrepresented the animal welfare position as one that ethically favors one species over another
(D) animal welfarism does not rely on utilitarianism
(E) the animal rights position cannot be right because it relies on a deontological view of animal ethics

181. The best response to the claim that causing animals unnecessary pain is wrong only because treating animals cruelly might cause us to treat human beings cruelly as well is to point out that _____.

(A) sometimes it is morally correct to treat human beings cruelly
(B) it is possible that animals do not actually experience pain or pleasure
(C) such thinking is speciesist
(D) this contradicts the common intuition that torturing animals would be wrong even if it did not degrade the moral character of the torturer
(E) treating animals cruelly is wrong because it violates the rights of animals

182. According to *deontological* approaches to animal ethics, how we treat animals depends on _____.

(A) what moral duties we have toward nonhuman animals

(B) how we can best maximize animal well-being

(C) what effect our treatment of animals might have on our ability to act morally toward human beings

(D) how animals treat us

(E) whether animals can feel pain

183. So-called marginal cases, such as severely brain-damaged infants, seem to present counterexamples to which claim?

(A) Animals do not have direct moral status because they lack uniquely human characteristics such as rationality and autonomy.

(B) Animals should be treated kindly only because cruelty of any kind is destructive to our moral being.

(C) Animals have rights that entail that they cannot be used as human property.

(D) Humans have no duties toward humans who lack rationality or free will.

(E) Species membership has no bearing on moral status.

184. Tom Regan argues in his influential book *The Case for Animal Rights* that some nonhuman animals have moral rights because they are *subjects-of-a(n)-*_____.

(A) *owner*

(B) *issue*

(C) *object*

(D) *life*

(E) *conscience*

Torture, Terrorism, and War

185. Which of the following descriptions is NOT a typical definition of *terrorism*?

(A) Harm perpetrated against innocent civilians with the intent to coerce through intimidation

(B) The intentional use of violence against noncombatants as a way to create fear and thereby effect a desired consequence

(C) A method of political intimidation involving violence or threats of violence against innocent civilians

(D) The use of military intimidation techniques against enemy combatants

(E) The use or attempted use of terror on civilians as a means of coercion

186. In his famous essay "Terrorism: A Critique of Excuses," Michael Walzer points out that _____.

(A) most people who condemn terrorism would practice it themselves, given the right circumstances

(B) most people neither advocate nor excuse terrorism

(C) while most people do not advocate terrorism, many do excuse it

(D) while they would not admit it, most people do not condemn terrorism

(E) some people use terrorism as an excuse for further terrorism

187. Some have argued that terrorism is generally to be condemned but that it is excusable in circumstances of "extreme emergency." Which of the following statements disagrees least with this claim?

(A) If terrorism involves the intentional killing of innocents, then no circumstances can be extreme enough to excuse it.

(B) There is an important distinction between *excusable* and *justified*.

(C) There is a slippery slope from "excusable in extreme circumstances" to "justified when those in power think it is."

(D) It is difficult to see who would be an appropriate judge as to whether circumstances constitute an "extreme emergency."

(E) Circumstances of "extreme emergency" that excuse terrorism do not actually arise, since there are always other viable options besides terrorism.

188. The claim that torture is justified if torturing produces (or is likely to produce) a greater balance of good effects over bad effects (than not torturing would) probably assumes which ethical view?

(A) Deontology
(B) Virtue ethics
(C) Contractarianism
(D) Consequentialism
(E) Relativism

189. The claim that torture is never justified because it goes against moral duties and basic human rights typically assumes which ethical view?

(A) Deontology
(B) Virtue ethics
(C) Contractarianism
(D) Consequentialism
(E) Relativism

190. Which of the following Latin phrases is often used in Just War Theory to denote the nature of just action *during* war?

(A) *jus ad bellum*
(B) *cogito ergo sum*
(C) *jus in bello*
(D) *esse est percipi*
(E) *ad hoc*

191. Apart from those who do not believe considerations of justice have any relevance to the politics of war, participants in the morality-of-war debate typically divide into which of the following two groups?

(A) Those who believe war can sometimes be just, and those who believe war is never just
(B) Those who believe war is just only if perpetrated by a sovereign nation, and those who believe war is just only if perpetrated by a democratic nation
(C) Liberals and conservatives
(D) Skeptics and realists
(E) Those who believe war is just only if innocent people do not suffer because of it, and those who believe war can be just even if innocent people suffer because of it

192. Which of the following is NOT one of the necessary conditions for a just war, as understood in Just War Theory?

(A) A state can resort to war only if all other reasonable means of ending conflict have been ruled out as live options.

(B) A state can resort to war only if it intends to wage war for the sake of a just cause and not for other reasons.

(C) A state can resort to war only if its citizens are unanimous in their agreement to war.

(D) A state can resort to war only if war is likely to bring about the desired outcome.

(E) A state can resort to war only if the goods expected from war are proportional to the ills expected from war.

193. The popular "clean hands" criticism of *pacifism* maintains that _____.

(A) pacifism must be wrong because there have been many just wars in the past

(B) a proponent of pacifism would neglect the duty to defend his or her nation merely in the name of remaining morally blameless

(C) pacifism must be wrong because there have never been any just wars in the past

(D) a proponent of pacifism is likely to accept aggressive protection against violence, despite his or her official stance of total nonviolence

(E) proponents of pacifism are likely to be unpatriotic or even treasonous

194. According to the *doctrine of double effect*, an action that has just or moral effects, but that also has unjust or immoral effects, is justified only if four criteria are met. Which of the following is NOT one of those criteria?

(A) The action must be one that is otherwise morally permissible.

(B) The agent performing the action must intend only the morally legitimate outcome of the action.

(C) The morally undesirable effect of the action must not be a means to the morally desirable effect of the action.

(D) Those directly affected by the action must give their consent to the action.

(E) The goodness caused by the action must outweigh the badness caused by the action.

195. Which two issues surrounding torture are typically held as being the main reasons for regarding torture as morally wrong?

(A) The physical pain inflicted on the victim and a typical loss of the victim's autonomy

(B) The brutalization of the torturer and the negative societal impact of torture

(C) The inefficacy of torture and the glorification of violence in Hollywood films

(D) The contradiction between torture and the Golden Rule, as well as the contradiction between torture and God's commandments

(E) The possibility of innocent victims and the likelihood of retaliation

196. It is often argued that torture ought to be legal (in extreme circumstances) since there are certain cases in which torturing someone is morally justified. How might one cogently respond to this argument?

(A) The connection between moral admissibility and a policy of legal admissibility needs to be established rather than simply assumed.

(B) The argument implicitly assumes that there is no distinction between *morally justified* and *morally excusable*.

(C) The argument relies on the unproven hypothesis that torturers are unlikely to become desensitized to the violence of torture.

(D) Since torture is in fact legal in many places, the argument is invalid.

(E) The argument relies on the truth of consequentialism.

197. Many of those who disapprove of legalized torture fear that the institutionalization of torture will lead to a(n) "_____ of torture."

(A) ritual

(B) worship

(C) nation

(D) atmosphere

(E) culture

198. In terms of settling on an appropriate definition of the word, one of the main problems with the way the word *terrorism* is commonly used is that _____.

(A) it is often used to refer to acts that are not strictly speaking acts of terrorism

(B) it is usually used to refer to acts of war in general

(C) it is typically used to refer to acts performed by nations other than one's own

(D) it is standardly used to refer to any acts of war that are unjust

(E) it is never used to refer to acts of violence against noncombatants

199. One who argues against torture on the basis of a fundamental duty not to intentionally curtail the autonomy of a human being characteristically relies on what view or theory of ethics?

(A) Virtue ethics
(B) Consequentialism
(C) Utilitarianism
(D) Deontology
(E) Ethical egoism

Poverty and Affluence

200. Who is the author of "Famine, Affluence, and Morality," the noteworthy 1971 article that argued that we have an obligation to donate much more money to charity than we typically think is appropriate?

(A) John Kekes
(B) Bertrand Russell
(C) Peter Singer
(D) Thomas Nagel
(E) Richard Rorty

201. Which of the following is a common objection to typical utilitarian views on charity?

(A) Donating money does not necessarily increase overall happiness.
(B) Utilitarianism entails an unrealistically high moral demand with regard to our obligations to donate to charities.
(C) It is impossible to calculate whether the overall balance between well-being and misery would be higher on account of charity donations.
(D) Utilitarianism does not always make the necessary distinction between *happiness* and *deserved happiness*.
(E) Utilitarianism falsely implies that donating to charity is wrong.

202. The notion of *beneficence* plays an important role in applied ethics. Which of the following is an apt definition for this notion?

(A) The common characteristic of all actions specifically intended to benefit others rather than oneself

(B) The common property of all beneficial actions

(C) A characteristic of any situation in which two competing parties benefit mutually from a harm done to a third party

(D) A moral rule that states that one must benefit others at least as much as one benefits oneself

(E) The sense of well-being one experiences as a result of acting altruistically

203. Which of the following is most easily recognized as an expression of a consequentialist view of the ethics of charity?

(A) It is important to develop all of one's virtues by practicing them. Being charitable is a virtue, so one ought to act charitably, at least sometimes.

(B) We have an absolute duty to practice beneficence. Not giving to charity violates this duty, and so one ought to give to charity.

(C) According to the Bible, it is important to feed the hungry and heal the sick. Donating to charity is the most direct means, short of actually working in relief, of doing so. Hence, we ought to give to charity.

(D) If everyone donated to charity all the time, it would become impossible to donate to charity. Thus, we have a duty *not* to donate to charity.

(E) It is possible to increase the well-being of many human beings by giving more to charity. Since we should always try to increase human well-being, we ought to give more to charity.

204. Which of the following is typically associated with the act or practice of benefiting someone without or against his or her consent?

(A) Charity

(B) Ethical egoism

(C) Feudalism

(D) Negative duty

(E) Paternalism

205. The principle of _____ states that it is sometimes morally permissible to benefit someone without his or her knowledge or consent.

(A) beneficence
(B) accord
(C) helping hands
(D) charity
(E) paternalism

206. The "ought implies can" objection to Singer's "Famine, Affluence, and Morality" essentially says that Singer's view on charity fails because _____.

(A) the notion that we *ought* to give more to charity than we normally do implies that the beneficiaries of the charities *can* become happier only with our aid
(B) it is wrong to help someone without his or her consent
(C) Singer's proposed moral standard is higher than we can reasonably expect people to meet, and so it cannot be the right moral standard
(D) it requires us to donate money even to the point of our own starvation and/or homelessness
(E) it is not fair that the beneficiaries of charity should benefit from the hard work of those who donate to charities

207. Which of the following denotes the concept of "going beyond the call of duty"?

(A) Beneficence
(B) Categorical imperative
(C) Supererogation
(D) Benevolence
(E) Principle of utility

208. The main argument given in Peter Singer's "Famine, Affluence, and Morality" relies on what theory of ethics?

(A) Social contract theory
(B) Consequentialism
(C) Feminist ethics
(D) Subjectivism
(E) Emotivism

209. Which of the following actions would typically be described as morally supererogatory rather than morally obligatory?

(A) Keeping a promise
(B) Abusing one's privileges
(C) Giving all one's belongings to a poor family
(D) Refraining from murder
(E) Stealing from the wealthy

210. According to John Kekes's critique of Singer's "Famine, Affluence, and Morality," Peter Singer's main position on charity _____.

(A) is based on rationally indefensible rampant moralism
(B) presents a noble idea but is impractical in reality
(C) does not adequately address the problem of paternalism
(D) creates an impossible-to-meet double standard
(E) is exactly correct, though the argument for it is flawed

211. In his writings about charity, Peter Singer claims that refraining from giving money to charity is _____.

(A) bad but not as bad as selling a child to organ peddlers
(B) justified because everyone has a right to his or her own income
(C) just as bad as selling a child to organ peddlers
(D) even worse than selling a child to organ peddlers
(E) not justified because charities do not force you to donate money against your will

212. It is sometimes argued, in the context of the ethics of charity, that there is a significant difference between my moral obligation to the homeless man on the other side of the street and my obligation to a starving mother on the other side of the planet. If someone disagreed with this claim, how might he or she plausibly reply to it?

(A) I cannot really be sure that the mother on the other side of the planet is actually starving.
(B) There is no difference at all between the two cases.
(C) If the claim were true, then I would never have moral obligations to those not in my proximity.
(D) While there is no way to deny this claim, I do not like it.
(E) There is no *morally* significant difference between the two cases, only a *psychological* difference.

213. Some have argued that one ought not to donate to privately run charities, as any kind of aid should be a government responsibility. Which of the following is a plausible critical response to this claim?

(A) The claim implies that all charity work ought to be done by government institutions.

(B) The claim assumes without support that government involvement will decrease as support for private charities increases.

(C) The claim is a red herring, since the real problem has to do with immigration.

(D) Privately run charities have every right to exist.

(E) Aid should be a government's responsibility.

214. Peter Singer's view on donating to charitable causes to help the poor is often criticized for being overly demanding. What is Singer's response to this critique?

(A) He denies that it is overly demanding; he thinks people could easily measure up to his moral standard if they would just try.

(B) He accepts the criticism and admits that his ideals are too stringent.

(C) He accepts the criticism but denies that it is fatal to his overall view.

(D) He denies that this is a relevant criticism, since his theory merely says what people *ought* to do, not what they will do.

(E) He denies that this is a relevant criticism, since it presumes a deontological framework of ethics, whereas he is working in a consequentialist tradition.

Euthanasia

215. Which of the following is NOT a classification of *euthanasia*?

(A) Assisted

(B) Voluntary

(C) Active

(D) Nonvoluntary

(E) Deliberate

216. Which of the following is the typical motivation for committing euthanasia?

(A) The desire of doctors to "play God"
(B) The desire to minimize suffering
(C) The desire to eventually institute a program of eugenics
(D) The desire of relatives to acquire the euthanized patient's inheritance
(E) The desire to get rid of sick people

217. Which is the best definition of *euthanasia* out of the options given?

(A) The act of one person taking the life of another person with the intention of putting an end to pointless suffering
(B) The movement advocating the killing of ill or disabled persons with the aim of purifying the gene pool
(C) The act of one person taking the life of another person against his or her will
(D) Not intervening when a person is about to die of natural causes
(E) The act of taking the life of another person with the intention of using that person's organs for medical research

218. Which of the following is NOT a typical argument against legalizing voluntary euthanasia?

(A) Today's medical science is able to provide excellent palliative care, rendering the need to end suffering through voluntary death unnecessary.
(B) Euthanasia fails the moral test of the doctrine of double effect.
(C) Euthanasia is bound to often and deeply upset the friends and family of the euthanized patient.
(D) We can never know for certain if a patient has really given his or her full, rational, and enduring consent.
(E) There is a slippery slope from legalizing voluntary euthanasia to practicing involuntary euthanasia.

219. Which of the following statements is most accurate?

(A) Euthanasia is legal in all of the United States.
(B) Euthanasia is legal in most of the United States.
(C) Euthanasia is legal in roughly half of the United States.
(D) Euthanasia is legal in only one state in the United States.
(E) Euthanasia is illegal in all of the United States.

220. It is sometimes argued that euthanasia fails the moral test of the doctrine of double effect. In what way might euthanasia fail this test?

(A) Euthanasia involves using something harmful in itself—namely, the taking of a life—in order to bring about something beneficial—the cessation of suffering.

(B) Euthanasia has a twofold effect on our moral character: it desensitizes us toward death and it destroys our sense of compassion.

(C) Euthanasia cannot be justified on the basis of any universal moral laws.

(D) Euthanasia is doubly immoral: it degrades the sanctity of life and disobeys God's laws.

(E) Euthanasia aims directly at something that is necessarily harmful to any human being: death.

221. It is often argued that while passive euthanasia might be morally justifiable, active euthanasia is not. What critical response is often given in reply?

(A) Although this is strictly speaking true, the real issue concerns only passive euthanasia.

(B) In fact, active euthanasia is morally justifiable, but passive euthanasia is not.

(C) This argument implies that the doctrine of double effect is false.

(D) The distinction between *active* and *passive* is morally insignificant in the context of discussions about euthanasia.

(E) The distinction between *morally justifiable* and *morally unjustifiable* is insignificant in the context of discussions about euthanasia.

222. According to the usual "slippery slope" argument against voluntary euthanasia, _____.

(A) the legalization of voluntary euthanasia will eventually cause doctors to perform involuntary euthanasia

(B) the legalization of voluntary euthanasia will eventually lead to a "culture of euthanasia"

(C) the legalization of voluntary euthanasia will eventually desensitize our culture to death

(D) the legalization of voluntary euthanasia is an affront to human dignity

(E) the legalization of voluntary euthanasia will eventually cause patients to seek death for no good reason

223. How might a supporter of legalized euthanasia reply to the claim that euthanasia ought not to be legalized because we can never know whether a patient has truly given his or her rational, informed, and enduring consent?

(A) The claim only shows that involuntary euthanasia should not be legalized.

(B) Although it is certainly true that we can never be sure whether patients have truly given their rational, informed, and enduring consent, the same could be said about anyone who has apparently given consent for something.

(C) The claim falsely implies that patients should not be believed when they say that they are in pain.

(D) The claim assumes that the interests of patients are best served by ignoring their requests.

(E) Although there will be some cases in which it is impossible to ascertain the quality of a patient's expressed consent, it is implausible to suppose that this knowledge would always be beyond reach.

224. To those who support legal euthanasia, what has seemed to be the main problem with the "slippery slope" argument against legalization?

(A) Slippery slope arguments are generally fallacious.

(B) There is no reliable empirical support to ground this argument.

(C) The argument implies that doctors are inherently attracted to death.

(D) The argument assumes that consequentialism is true.

(E) It is wrong to suppose that the issue of euthanasia has anything to do with a slippery slope situation.

225. The claim that euthanasia is morally acceptable whenever it creates a higher overall balance of well-being over misery relies on what view of ethics?

(A) Psychological egoism

(B) Ethical behaviorism

(C) Moral realism

(D) Consequentialism

(E) Divine command theory

226. Those who advocate legalization of euthanasia often offer criteria that must be met by any legitimate candidate for euthanasia. Which of the following is NOT one of those?

(A) The patient is suffering from a terminal illness.
(B) The patient is extremely unlikely to be suddenly cured.
(C) The patient has expressed a voluntary, sane, and enduring request for euthanasia.
(D) The patient has no close family members who object to the euthanasia.
(E) The patient cannot commit suicide without assistance.

227. How might a supporter of legalized euthanasia reply to the claim that euthanasia ought not to be legalized because today's medical science is able to provide excellent palliative care, rendering the need to end suffering through voluntary death unnecessary?

(A) Even with today's advanced pain management options, patients still make the judgment that the pain and/or loss of autonomy associated with the illness makes life not worth living.
(B) Homeopathic remedies are far superior to Western medical science.
(C) Even today's advanced pain management options do not help the patient's cognitive functions.
(D) Advances in medical science may make euthanasia *immoral*, but that does not mean it should also be *illegal*.
(E) The need to end suffering through voluntary death is unnecessary anyway.

228. A critique of the legalization of euthanasia based on a *deontological* view of ethics might make which of the following claims?

(A) Euthanasia, if legalized, would *decrease* happiness rather than increase it.
(B) According to the Bible, euthanasia is immoral.
(C) We have an absolute duty never to take the life of an innocent person.
(D) The practice of euthanasia destroys the virtuous character trait of empathy.
(E) The legalization of euthanasia would result in widespread immorality and depravity.

229. Perhaps no real-life case is as well known for causing widespread controversy surrounding euthanasia as _____.

(A) Roe v. Wade
(B) the Terri Schiavo case
(C) the Schrieffer case
(D) the case of Charles Dexter Ward
(E) Miranda v. Arizona

Abortion

230. The most common argument against abortion is that _____.

(A) abortion is not an effective method of birth control
(B) women should not have sex if they do not want to get pregnant
(C) a fetus is a human person with all the rights of a human person
(D) abortion is not good for society as a whole
(E) abortion is based on an ancient, barbaric tradition of killing unwanted children

231. Which of the following is the name of the 1973 landmark U.S. Supreme Court case that resulted in the striking down of abortion-banning laws?

(A) Kramer v. Kramer
(B) Scopes v. State
(C) Roe v. Wade
(D) Miranda v. Arizona
(E) Gideon v. Wainright

232. The abortion debate tends to center around which philosophically interesting concept?

(A) Consciousness
(B) Just deserts
(C) Rights
(D) Intentionality
(E) Nature

233. Which of the following traits is NOT typically thought of as a defining, essential human trait?

(A) Autonomy
(B) Rationality
(C) Morality
(D) Self-consciousness
(E) Originality

234. Don Marquis's famous 1989 article "Why Abortion Is Immoral" primarily makes which claim about abortion?

(A) Abortion is wrong because a fetus is a person.
(B) Abortion is wrong because God has revealed it to be so.
(C) Abortion is wrong because it deprives a potential mother of a child.
(D) Abortion is wrong because it is an effect of male patriarchy.
(E) Abortion is wrong because it deprives a being of a future of value.

235. Who authored the landmark 1971 paper "A Defense of Abortion"?

(A) Judith Jarvis Thomson
(B) Don Marquis
(C) Mary Anne Warren
(D) Peter Singer
(E) Ronald Dworkin

236. Suppose someone disapproved of abortion on the grounds that abortion causes a greater balance of misery over well-being than refraining from abortion. What ethical theory or view does this disapproval presuppose?

(A) Consequentialism
(B) Virtue ethics
(C) Moral realism
(D) Moral relativism
(E) Moral nihilism

237. The abortion debate is often seen as essentially a debate about when personhood begins. How does the paper "Why Abortion Is Immoral" question this public perception?

(A) It argues instead that abortion robs a fetus, person or not, of an absolute value.
(B) It argues instead that abortion is sometimes justified because refusing to let a being, person or not, use one's body as a lifesaving mechanism is justified.
(C) It argues instead that abortion is never justified because allowing a being, person or not, to use one's body as a lifesaving mechanism is never justified.
(D) It argues instead that abortion kills a fetus, person or not.
(E) It argues instead that abortion is wrong because it involves the murder of a person with rights.

238. According to the argument given in the 1971 paper "A Defense of Abortion," the right to life does not entail _____.

(A) the right to use another person's body to preserve one's own life
(B) the right to defend oneself against unjustified attacks
(C) the privilege of life
(D) the privilege of abortion
(E) the right to kill

239. Some have claimed that the argument that abortion is wrong because it deprives a being of a future of value must be unsound because it entails the absurd conclusion that contraception must then also be wrong. How might one plausibly respond to this criticism on behalf of the position under attack?

(A) The conclusion is not absurd at all: contraception *is* wrong.
(B) Neither the egg nor the sperm has a future of value before they are joined.
(C) The egg doesn't need any *particular* sperm to fertilize it.
(D) Contraception actually *enables* beings to have futures of values.
(E) Contraception is not wrong.

240. The abortion debate is often seen as essentially a debate about when personhood begins. How does the famous 1971 paper "A Defense of Abortion" question this public perception?

(A) It argues instead that abortion is wrong because it involves the murder of a person with rights.
(B) It argues instead that abortion is sometimes justified because refusing to let a being, person or not, use one's body as a lifesaving mechanism is justified.
(C) It argues instead that abortion robs a fetus, person or not, of an absolute value.
(D) It argues instead that abortion kills a fetus, person or not.
(E) It argues instead that abortion is never justified, because allowing a being, person or not, to use one's body as a lifesaving mechanism is never justified.

241. Judith Jarvis Thomson is responsible for the influential "famous violinist" thought experiment. According to Thomson, it would be _____ to refrain from unplugging the violinist.

(A) nice, but not obligatory
(B) justified, but not beneficent
(C) excusable, but not justified
(D) terrible, but funny
(E) predictable, but not inevitable

242. In his article "Why Abortion Is Immoral," Don Marquis considers several proposed answers to the question "Why is murder wrong?" Which of the following is one of those answers?

(A) Murder constitutes a breach of the Golden Rule.
(B) Murder does not maximize well-being.
(C) Murder is not virtuous.
(D) Murder is condemned in the Bible.
(E) Murder brutalizes the murderer.

243. In response to Judith Jarvis Thomson's thought experiment drawing an analogy between pregnancy and being attached intravenously to another person dependent upon your blood for survival, critics argue that there is a significant disanalogy between the two cases in that _____.

(A) the pregnancy case is very realistic, whereas the "intravenous attachment" case would never happen in real life
(B) the pregnancy case involves an unborn baby, whereas the "intravenous attachment" case involves a fully grown violinist
(C) neither case explicitly mentions who the father is supposed to be, either literally or analogically
(D) both cases involve having a living creature depend on someone else for its life
(E) there is typically (apart from cases of rape) some culpability on the part of a woman who becomes pregnant, whereas the "intravenous attachment" case does not involve similar culpability

244. Some have pointed out the asymmetry between women's and men's legal obligations concerning parenthood. These critics maintain that the fact that men can easily and without legal repercussion "walk out" on parenthood creates a(n) _____.

(A) atmosphere of intimidation
(B) double standard
(C) culture of compliance
(D) safety measure
(E) patriarchy of absence

Bioethics

245. Which of the following is the name of the highly influential and first-ever American textbook on bioethics?

(A) *De Humani Corporis Fabrica*
(B) *Bioethics: An Introduction*
(C) *Biological Science and Morality*
(D) *The Descent of Man*
(E) *Principles of Biomedical Ethics*

246. Which of the following controversial topics would not fall under the purview of bioethics?

(A) Cloning
(B) Euthanasia
(C) Abortion
(D) Creationism
(E) Stem cell research

247. The oath typically taken by health-care professionals swearing to practice medicine ethically is called _____.

(A) the Care Contract
(B) the Vow of Ethical Practice
(C) the Hippocratic oath
(D) the Oath of Fealty
(E) Patient-Doctor Confidentiality

248. Which of the following is an accurate definition of *bioethics*?
   (A) A theory that reduces morality to biological imperatives
   (B) A field of study dedicated to creating ethical theories on the basis of modern understanding of biology
   (C) A theory of ethics meant to solve any ethical issues that arise in the areas of medicine and biology
   (D) A field of research dedicated to gathering empirical data about the way biological beings behave ethically
   (E) A field of study dedicated to thinking about and analyzing ethical issues that arise in the areas of medicine and biology

249. Which of the following is NOT one of the typical values referred to in discussions of medical ethics?
   (A) Autonomy
   (B) Nonmaleficence
   (C) Punctuality
   (D) Justice
   (E) Dignity

250. When a patient has full understanding of the potential benefits and risks of a proposed course of treatment and makes a sane, voluntary decision to submit to the treatment, that decision is typically called _____.
   (A) dignified response
   (B) informed consent
   (C) a double effect
   (D) autonomous action
   (E) a moral choice

251. Which of the following is widely regarded as the cornerstone document of research ethics?
   (A) The Declaration of Helsinki
   (B) The Monroe Doctrine
   (C) Science and Engineering Ethics
   (D) Publication Ethical Standards: Guidelines and Procedures
   (E) Professional Ethics Report

252. Baby K, the baby born with only a brain stem who was kept alive artificially for religious reasons, caused much controversy in the field of bioethics. Which of the following concepts was NOT one of those brought under scrutiny by the case?

(A) Sanctity of life
(B) Autonomy
(C) Quality of life
(D) Just deserts
(E) Personhood

253. Which of the following best gives the meaning of *nonmaleficence*?

(A) The "first do no harm" principle
(B) The utilitarian principle
(C) The nonexistence of evil
(D) The property or characteristic of all actions that are not aimed at maximizing well-being
(E) The property or characteristic of all actions that are aimed at minimizing the autonomy of the patient

254. Which of the following is NOT a typical stance on the ethics of stem cell research?

(A) Human embryos should under no conditions be harmed, even to save lives.
(B) Human embryos deserve more respect than a mere cluster of cells, but sometimes their destruction is justified.
(C) Human embryos should be destroyed only when they become useless to research.
(D) Human embryos are merely a cluster of cells, lacking the status of human personhood.
(E) Human embryos that are clones may be destroyed, but not the source embryo.

255. Which of the following is NOT one of the four principles of *principlism*?

(A) Beneficence
(B) Supererogation
(C) Autonomy
(D) Nonmaleficence
(E) Justice

256. Opponents of human cloning often claim that a clone's identity or autonomy is endangered by the fact of having a genotype that has already existed. Which of the following claims best addresses this concern?

(A) Free will is an illusion.

(B) If this claim is true, then *any* person's identity or autonomy is threatened on similar grounds.

(C) It is always possible to destroy the original genotype.

(D) This claim falsely assumes that personal identity is determined entirely by genotype.

(E) Questions about personal identity are best answered by studying human biology.

257. What is the *doctrine of double effect*?

(A) The set of principles that determine the outcome of any overdetermined event

(B) A set of criteria for the ethical evaluation of actions that have both morally positive and morally negative effects

(C) The principle according to which there is an equal and opposite reaction to every action

(D) The teaching according to which we should always think twice about our actions

(E) A set of criteria for the ethical evaluation of actions that involve both a physical and a mental component

258. One of the principal values of medical ethics, *autonomy*, concerns

_____.

(A) the right of any patient to self-determination and free choice with regard to medical treatment

(B) the right of any patient to the protection of basic human freedoms

(C) the medical practice of treating patients as though they are business clients

(D) the tendency of patients to think that they know better than the doctor does

(E) the right of any patient to have access to treatment, regardless of whether the disease has been caused by the patient's own choices

Affirmative Action

259. Critics have claimed that affirmative action, when effected through preferential selection, confounds justice in a variety of ways. Which of the following is NOT one of those?

(A) It is not clear whether those affected positively by preferential selection *deserve* those benefits.

(B) Those most deserving of jobs sometimes will not get them because of their race.

(C) Justice cannot be achieved by making those not responsible for a social ill pay for it.

(D) Those who are most negatively affected by preferential selection are typically too young to have enjoyed the unfair advantage given to whites because of slavery.

(E) Employers are unjustly made to change the status quo, even if the status quo has been good for the employer.

260. *Affirmative action* refers to _____.

(A) policies that take factors such as race, religion, gender, sexual orientation, etc., into consideration, with the aim of benefiting an underrepresented group in order to counter the effects of a history of discrimination

(B) policies that ignore factors such as race, religion, gender, sexual orientation, etc., in hiring procedures, with the aim of removing arbitrary personal traits from the list of relevant skills and talents required for the job

(C) policies that mandate, by law, racial segregation in all public facilities, with a so-called separate but equal status for black Americans

(D) policies that outlaw major forms of discrimination against blacks and women, including racial segregation

(E) policies that ensure financial compensation for the descendants of slaves as a way to make up for the coerced and uncompensated labor performed by their ancestors

261. Critics often see affirmative action as a special form of discrimination, referred to as _____.

    (A) a double standard
    (B) segregation
    (C) institutionalized racism
    (D) reverse racism
    (E) a quota system

262. Suppose someone argued that the effects of affirmative action would involve a decrease in the overall balance of well-being over misery, and so affirmative action is wrong. What system or view of ethics underlies this argument?

    (A) Deontology
    (B) Virtue ethics
    (C) Moral nihilism
    (D) Emotivism
    (E) Consequentialism

263. Which of the following is an apt description of *preferential selection* in the context of affirmative action?

    (A) Selection of a person for hiring or acceptance into college on the basis of race, gender, ethnicity, etc.
    (B) Selection of a person for hiring or acceptance into college on the basis of relevant skills and abilities
    (C) Selection of a special interest group for public acknowledgment of their special abilities and talents
    (D) Selection of any person to receive special grants for business and education
    (E) Selection of a person for public acknowledgment of his or her special abilities and talents

264. What ethical notion is central to the argument in James Rachels's "What People Deserve"?

    (A) Just deserts
    (B) Happiness
    (C) Love
    (D) The categorical imperative
    (E) The hedonistic calculus

265. How might one respond to the charge that affirmative action is no more than an attempt at social engineering by liberal Democrats?

    (A) Liberal Democrats have traditionally stayed away from social engineering.

    (B) Affirmative action is actually an attempt at social engineering by conservative Republicans.

    (C) Lyndon Johnson's Executive Order 11246 was the originating document of affirmative action programs in the United States.

    (D) Affirmative action programs have not had the results that they were supposed to have had, and there is no longer any reason to continue support for them.

    (E) Affirmative action programs have been in place under the administrations of three Democratic presidents and *six* Republican presidents.

266. Which of the following is NOT one of the main criticisms of affirmative action?

    (A) Affirmative action enforces an unjust "quota" system.

    (B) Affirmative action rewards those who do not themselves deserve reward.

    (C) Affirmative action punishes those who do not themselves deserve punishment.

    (D) Affirmative action only works if those affected by it do not harbor resentment toward one another as a result of it.

    (E) Affirmative action involves "reverse racism."

267. The policy that has usually been responsible for the greatest opposition to affirmative action measures is _____.

    (A) neutrality

    (B) deliberate ambiguity

    (C) tolerance

    (D) undifferentiated potential

    (E) preferential selection

268. Which American president signed into law Executive Order 10925, the order that first introduced the term *affirmative action*?

    (A) J. Edgar Hoover

    (B) John F. Kennedy

    (C) Abraham Lincoln

    (D) Richard Nixon

    (E) Dwight D. Eisenhower

269. How might one plausibly respond to one who argues that affirmative action "quota" policies are unfair because they involve hiring unqualified persons merely on the basis of race or sex?

    (A) There have never existed any quota policies.
    (B) So-called quota policies are not meant to result in the hiring of unqualified persons on the basis of race or sex, but are meant only to ensure that qualified people of all groups are equally represented.
    (C) So-called quota policies are fair, since they benefit social groups who have suffered discrimination in the past.
    (D) The reason that hiring an unqualified person not on the basis of his or her abilities is justified in the context of affirmative action is that the unqualified person has suffered because of past discrimination.
    (E) Affirmative action is meant to address a social problem, not to manage the subtleties of the workplace.

270. A purported negative effect of affirmative action is *mismatching*. Which of the following describes this effect?

    (A) Minority groups being "reversely" discriminated against.
    (B) Employees being placed in jobs that do not make them enough money.
    (C) Students being placed in colleges that are too difficult for them.
    (D) Employers being stuck with employees who do not have the correct qualifications.
    (E) Students being placed in colleges that are too easy for them.

271. So-called Rawlsian justifications of affirmative action involve what core Rawlsian ethical notion?

    (A) Just deserts
    (B) Goodness as a natural property
    (C) Moral equality
    (D) The hedonistic paradox
    (E) Justice as fairness

CHAPTER 4

Political Philosophy

Plato and Aristotle

272. Which of the following constituents form Plato's imagined state?

(A) The producing class, the bourgeoisie, and the governing class
(B) The priestly class, the middle class, and the proletariat
(C) The middle class, the lower class, and the upper class
(D) The governing class, the guardian class, and the producing class
(E) The guardian class, the producing class, and the priestly class

273. Thrasymachus's view, as presented in Plato's most famous political treatise, can best be described as the view that _____.

(A) if God is dead, everything is permitted
(B) might makes right
(C) leaders have a sacred duty toward their subjects
(D) he who lives by the sword dies by the sword
(E) women have no place in politics

274. Which of the following dialogues of Plato is famous for its discussion of politics and law?

(A) *The Meno*
(B) *The Republic*
(C) *The Apology*
(D) *Laches*
(E) *The Euthyphro*

275. According to Socrates, as presented in Plato's dialogues, the distinction between male and female _____.

    (A) justifies treating women like slaves

    (B) is an absolute, God-given distinction

    (C) is akin to the distinction between human and animal

    (D) represents an absolute social distinction

    (E) is irrelevant when it comes to the assignment of education and jobs

276. Which of the following is NOT a main criticism of Plato's vision of the perfect state?

    (A) It is overly feminist.

    (B) It is overly totalitarian.

    (C) It is overly utopian.

    (D) It is overly communist.

    (E) It is overly antidemocratic.

277. According to Plato's vision of the ideal society, the ruling classes ought to have _____.

    (A) more money and luxury than the ruled class

    (B) special privileges not available to the ruled class

    (C) less money and luxury than the ruled class

    (D) less propensity for intellectual thought than the ruled class

    (E) the same amount of money and luxury as the ruled class

278. According to Plato, the composition of his ideal state is analogous to the composition of _____.

    (A) Athens

    (B) the state of nature

    (C) the soul

    (D) the Realm of the Good

    (E) mathematical forms

279. Which of the following are the respective goals of Plato's philosopher, guardian, and producer?

    (A) Wisdom, honor, wealth

    (B) Honor, peace, wealth

    (C) Love, peace, happiness

    (D) Wisdom, wealth, happiness

    (E) Happiness, power, wealth

280. Which of the following is NOT a feature of Plato's ideal state?

(A) Equal consideration of men and women for job and educational opportunities

(B) Obliteration of private property for the ruled class

(C) Propaganda aimed at the good of the state

(D) Censorship of certain forms of art

(E) State-sponsored education

281. To Polemarchus's definition of justice, Plato has Socrates give what counterexample?

(A) Returning a runaway slave to his master

(B) Giving taxes to a tyrant

(C) Giving a child an adult task

(D) Giving charity to a poor person

(E) Giving a mentally deranged person his axe back

282. What ability does Plato's imagined "ring of Gyges" bestow upon its bearer?

(A) Immortality

(B) Invisibility

(C) Omnipotence

(D) Perfect virtue

(E) Popularity

283. According to Plato, whether one becomes a ruler, guardian, or producer is determined _____.

(A) entirely by heredity

(B) typically by heredity, but personal capacity is the final determinant

(C) by a lottery

(D) by what an individual decides at the beginning of adulthood

(E) by what an individual's parents decide

284. Which of the following is NOT a definition of *justice* proposed in *The Republic*?

(A) Speaking the truth and repaying debts

(B) Benefiting friends and harming enemies

(C) Benefiting the just and harming the unjust

(D) The advantage of the stronger

(E) The instruction of the law

285. Aristotle describes his subject matter in the *Nicomachean Ethics* as ——————.

(A) ethics
(B) political science
(C) political philosophy
(D) rhetoric
(E) logic

286. Aristotle often compares the politician to a(n) ——————.

(A) ethicist
(B) judge
(C) craftsman
(D) rhetorician
(E) scientist

287. Aristotle conceives of a constitution as a(n) ——————.

(A) organizing principle
(B) written document
(C) mere formality
(D) product of consensus
(E) perfect idea

288. Aristotle thought that slavery was justified because ——————.

(A) the stronger has the right to rule over the weaker
(B) those who are masters need extra help
(C) there is no evidence to the contrary
(D) slaves naturally need a master to direct their lives
(E) slaves captured as spoils of war are naturally owned by the victors

289. According to Aristotle, the dominant class in an oligarchy is usually ——————.

(A) the noble
(B) the divinely appointed
(C) the culturally refined
(D) the wealthy
(E) the intelligentsia

290. What kind of political system did Aristotle think was optimal?

(A) A democracy
(B) An aristocracy
(C) An oligarchy
(D) A monarchy
(E) Anarchy

291. According to Aristotle, the end goal of the city-state is _____.

(A) the promotion of liberty and equality
(B) the maximization of wealth
(C) to grow in population
(D) to conquer lesser city-states
(E) the promotion of the virtues

292. In what kind of situation did Aristotle concede that democracy might be a good thing?

(A) If more people pooled together were more virtuous together than separately
(B) If a learned aristocracy had veto power over the decisions of the democrats
(C) If the general level of education of people were raised
(D) If women and slaves were both allowed to participate
(E) If term limits were placed on those elected to public office

293. During which time period did Plato write?

(A) The first half of the 4th century BCE
(B) The second half of the 4th century BCE
(C) The first half of the 3rd century BCE
(D) The second half of the 3rd century BCE
(E) The 2nd century BCE

294. During which time period did Aristotle write?

(A) The first half of the 4th century BCE
(B) The second half of the 4th century BCE
(C) The first half of the 3rd century BCE
(D) The second half of the 3rd century BCE
(E) The 2nd century BCE

Thomas Hobbes and John Locke

295. According to Hobbes, humans agree to live according to certain social rules in order to escape what he calls _____.

(A) sovereignty by acquisition
(B) the leviathan
(C) a state of tyranny
(D) a state of nature
(E) a social contract

296. Which of the following definitions is the most apt for describing *social contract theory* in the context of political philosophy?

(A) The theory according to which legitimate political authority is derived from the mutual consent of the governed
(B) The theory according to which laws are legitimate only if they are explicitly consented to by the governed
(C) A model of government according to which the governing body can be likened to the rational part of the human psyche
(D) An idealized model of government wherein the working class is always fairly represented by individuals in the governing body
(E) The theory according to which legitimate monarchs must sign a contract swearing obeisance to the will of the governed

297. According to Hobbes, absolute monarchy is the only viable form of government because _____.

(A) government here on earth ought to be a reflection of government in heaven, where God presides as absolute king over all creation
(B) it is the only form of government that demands absolute obedience from its subjects
(C) people crave and need unquestioned leadership
(D) the only other alternative, democracy, depends for its survival on the intelligence of the voters, which is not something we can count on
(E) it is the only form of government not systematically prone to dissolution through civil war

298. Hobbes is known for his description of a process whereby individuals unite into political societies. This process is often described as entering into a _____.

(A) social contract
(B) state of nature
(C) tacit consent
(D) condition of war
(E) politicization of states

299. The book in which Hobbes presents his influential political philosophy is called _____.

(A) *The Republic*
(B) *The Social Contract*
(C) *A Theory of Justice*
(D) *Leviathan*
(E) *Nicomachean Ethics*

300. Which of the following is NOT one of the 12 principal rights had by Hobbes's absolute sovereign?

(A) To wage war as he sees fit
(B) Not to be put to death by his subjects
(C) To create civil and property laws
(D) Not to be prevented from changing the covenant that forms the commonwealth
(E) To choose his counselors, ministers, magistrates, and officers

301. Which of the following best describes Locke's view on the types of government that are possible?

(A) Six types are possible: monarchy, tyranny, aristocracy, oligarchy, democracy, and anarchy.
(B) Three types are possible: monarchy, oligarchy, and anarchy, which is why monarchy is the preferred form of government.
(C) Three types are possible: monarchy, aristocracy, and democracy. Tyranny, oligarchy, and anarchy are merely defective or unpopular forms of monarchy, aristocracy, and democracy (respectively).
(D) Two types are possible: democracy and anarchy, which is why democracy is the preferred form of government.
(E) Only one type is possible: monarchy. All other types are merely forms of anarchy, which is the absence of, rather than a form of, government.

302. In his political philosophy, John Locke famously distinguished between
_____.

(A) divine law and human law
(B) national law and international law
(C) natural law and conventional law
(D) law by consent and law by force
(E) law of the people and law for the people

303. It can be argued that Locke's *Two Treatises* distinguishes among four
basic duties. Which of the following is NOT one of them?

(A) A duty to preserve oneself
(B) A duty to preserve others, when this doesn't conflict with the duty
to preserve oneself
(C) A duty not to destroy others
(D) A duty not to act in a way that conflicts with the happiness of others
(E) A duty not to act in a way that has a tendency to destroy others

304. Locke's *Two Treatises* presents a political theory based on _____.

(A) utilitarianism and divine law
(B) the detailed account of applied politics given in Machiavelli's
The Prince
(C) anarchy and libertarianism
(D) the ideal state described in Plato's *Republic*
(E) social contract theory and natural rights theory

305. Which of the following best describes Locke's views on the relation
between the justification of government and the appeal to the divine
right of kings?

(A) A government can be justified only by an appeal to the divine right
of kings.
(B) The divine right of kings shows that monarchy is always a justified
form of government.
(C) A government can never be justified by an appeal to the divine right
of kings.
(D) The fact that kings do not have divine right shows that monarchy
is never a justified form of government.
(E) A government can sometimes be justified by an appeal to the divine
right of kings.

306. Which of the following premises does Locke appeal to in order to defend the right to private property?

(A) The right to ownership of our own bodies extends to the right to ownership of the labor of our bodies and the effects of that labor.

(B) God, in His divine wisdom, ensures that property is distributed fairly, each person receiving what is his due.

(C) If property were only public, then each would lay equal claim to property, and anarchy would ensue.

(D) Without the possibility of the acquisition of personal property, there would be no motivation to work.

(E) Individuals may enter into a mutual contract ensuring the right to private property.

307. Which of the following is NOT one of the political notions argued for by Locke?

(A) The right of revolution

(B) The right of personal property

(C) The necessity of a social contract to escape the state of nature

(D) The divine right of kings

(E) Equal rights for all individuals

308. In what year was Thomas Hobbes's *Leviathan* published?

(A) 1596

(B) 1602

(C) 1651

(D) 1748

(E) 1805

309. In what year was John Locke's *Two Treatises of Government* published?

(A) 1542

(B) 1602

(C) 1648

(D) 1689

(E) 1777

J. S. Mill and John Rawls

310. Mill's vision of ethics and politics is mostly based on a specific type of which general approach to ethics?

(A) Deontology
(B) Virtue ethics
(C) Consequentialism
(D) Divine command theory
(E) Relativism

311. For what purpose, and only that purpose, does Mill claim that individuals' liberty may be legitimately restricted against their will?

(A) To compel them to follow the law
(B) To prevent them from harming others
(C) To cause them the pain that they caused others
(D) To make them see the error of their ways
(E) To ensure justice through equal retribution

312. Which of the following claims is NOT used by Mill to defend freedom of expression?

(A) An expressed opinion, even if unpalatable to some, may still be true.
(B) An expressed opinion, even if false, may still contain some truth.
(C) An expressed opinion, even if lacking in truth altogether, may still prevent true opinions from becoming dogma.
(D) A true opinion, if it becomes a dogma because alternate opinions are censored, becomes meaningless.
(E) A true opinion, if expressed to an agreeable audience, would not lead to censorship.

313. Mill labels the social phenomenon of a majority group limiting the freedoms of a minority group _____.

(A) a violation of the harm principle
(B) paternalism
(C) the herd instinct
(D) the tyranny of the majority
(E) a natural right

314. Which of the following best describes Mill's views on liberty?
- (A) Liberty is the freedom to do whatever one wants.
- (B) Liberty is the state of not being enslaved.
- (C) Liberty is the natural human capacity to make free choices.
- (D) Liberty is truly possible only for a select few.
- (E) Liberty is the right to do whatever does not harm others.

315. The practice of limiting people's freedom for their own good is for Mill
_____.
- (A) an instance of paternalism, and should be encouraged
- (B) an instance of paternalism, and should be avoided
- (C) an instance of supererogation, and should be avoided
- (D) an instance of moralism, and should be avoided
- (E) an instance of moralism, and should be encouraged

316. The political philosopher John Rawls is perhaps best known for his influential work _____.
- (A) *The Social Contract*
- (B) *Leviathan*
- (C) *The Republic*
- (D) *A Theory of Justice*
- (E) *Republicanism: A Theory of Freedom and Government*

317. Rawls's theoretical device the "veil of ignorance" involves imagining
_____.
- (A) a society in which the effects of one's actions are never known
- (B) a society in which other individuals' motivations are never known
- (C) that one lives in a society that does not recognize one's basic human rights
- (D) the construction of a society while one is unaware of the social role one will have in this society (with regard to things such as race, religion, sex, disability, etc.)
- (E) the construction of a society wherein one acts in a way that is blind to the social roles of others (with regard to things such as race, religion, sex, disability, etc.)

318. Rawls's theory of social justice takes as its basis the notion of justice as _____.

(A) liberty
(B) a basic right
(C) fairness
(D) a categorical imperative
(E) utility

319. Which of the following best describes Rawls's view of the kind of principles that would govern a maximally just society?

(A) They are those principles that free, rational, and equal people would agree to live by, under the condition that others live by these as well.
(B) They are those principles that, when followed, tend to produce greater human happiness than other principles.
(C) They are those principles that produce no inconsistencies when they are imagined to be followed by all individuals.
(D) They are those principles that have a tendency to maximize personal liberty and minimize political power over personal liberty.
(E) They are those principles that the majority of a population would agree to live by, under the condition that the minority would live by them as well.

320. Which of the following is NOT a well-known criticism of Rawls's theory of justice?

(A) The theory does not take into account the existence of natural rights.
(B) The theory fails to account for the injustices found in patriarchal social relations.
(C) The theory functions essentially as a defense for the status quo, without adequately addressing the social injustices found therein.
(D) The theory fails to give an adequate treatment of those aspects of game theory that deal with human psychology.
(E) The theory fails to show that Rawls's "two Principles of Justice" follow from his conception of justice as fairness.

321. Rawls's hypothetical situation (behind the "veil of ignorance") from within which individuals imagine the principles that will determine the social structure of their society is known as the _____.

(A) state of nature
(B) myth of Er
(C) social contract
(D) hedonistic calculus
(E) original position

322. According to Rawls's difference principle, _____.
- (A) social and economic differences tend to bring the greatest benefit to the most advantaged
- (B) religious and moral differences ought to bring the least benefit to those who are the most advantaged
- (C) religious and moral differences ought to bring the greatest benefit to those who are correct
- (D) social and economic inequalities ought to bring the greatest benefit to the most deserving
- (E) social and economic inequalities ought to bring the greatest benefit to the least advantaged

323. Which of the following is NOT one of Rawls's primary goods?
- (A) Basic rights and liberties
- (B) Freedom of movement and choice of occupation
- (C) Freedom to forfeit one's own basic rights
- (D) The social bases of self-respect
- (E) Income and wealth

324. In what year was J. S. Mill's *On Liberty* published?
- (A) 1820
- (B) 1859
- (C) 1896
- (D) 1904
- (E) 1948

325. In what year was John Rawls's *A Theory of Justice* first published?
- (A) 1879
- (B) 1938
- (C) 1951
- (D) 1962
- (E) 1971

CHAPTER 5

Philosophy of Religion

God and Religious Belief

326. Which of the following is NOT typically thought of as a characteristic of the traditional God of monotheism?

(A) Omnipotence
(B) Transcendence of laws of physics
(C) Omniscience
(D) Transcendence of laws of logic
(E) Omnibenevolence

327. The main difference between a *theist* and a *deist* could be said to be that _____.

(A) a theist believes that God may continue to influence and act in the universe after having created it, while a deist believes that God does not intervene in the universe after having created it
(B) a theist believes that God exists within time, while a deist believes that God exists outside of time
(C) a theist believes that God definitely exists, while a deist only thinks it probable
(D) a theist believes that God's existence can be demonstrated by reason, while a deist believes that God's existence is purely a matter of faith
(E) a theist believes that God's existence is compatible with unnecessary suffering, while a deist believes that God does not exist if unnecessary suffering exists

328. The belief that God is identical with the universe is known as
_____.

(A) dualism
(B) deism
(C) mind-body identity
(D) naturalism
(E) pantheism

329. According to _____, one can talk about God only in terms
of what God is *not*.

(A) monotheism
(B) deism
(C) negative theology
(D) logical positivism
(E) Christianity

330. The main point of *reformed epistemology*, as proposed by thinkers such
as Alvin Plantinga and William Alston, is that _____.

(A) a rational belief in God does not require an inference from other
truths
(B) theism is the only worldview that accounts for the very possibility
of knowledge
(C) belief in God requires justification on independent grounds
(D) disbelief in God occurs because of sin
(E) atheism is the only viable belief system in a post-Darwinian world

331. Which term most accurately describes a person who believes that the
existence or nonexistence of God cannot be known?

(A) Atheist
(B) Skeptic
(C) Naturalist
(D) Scientist
(E) Agnostic

332. Which of the following best describes the meaning of *fideism*?

(A) It is to deism what atheism is to theism
(B) A version of deism that does not deny the Trinity
(C) The theory that faith is more suited than rationality for arriving
at certain truths
(D) A version of deism that holds that although God does not intervene
in the world, He is still immanent
(E) The theory that faith is not required for justified belief in God

333. Which of the following statements best describes the logical relation between theism, atheism, and agnosticism?

(A) They are mutually incompatible.
(B) Atheism is compatible with agnosticism, but not with theism.
(C) Theism is compatible with agnosticism, but not with atheism.
(D) Agnosticism is compatible with both theism and atheism.
(E) They are all compatible.

334. Which of the following options accurately lists the titles of the two documents, written by W. K. Clifford and William James, respectively, that are typically thought of as the foundation of subsequent discussions concerning the "ethics of belief"?

(A) *Meditations on First Philosophy* and *Critique of Pure Reason*
(B) *Essence of Christianity* and *The Will to Power*
(C) *The Will to Power* and *The Will to Believe*
(D) *The Ethics of Belief* and *The Will to Believe*
(E) *The God Delusion* and *God Is Not Great: How Religion Poisons Everything*

335. According to William James, we have the right to believe something for which we have inadequate evidence when the belief is _____.

(A) comforting, widely shared, and commonsensical
(B) intelligible, consistent, and reasonable
(C) true, logical, and desirable
(D) live, forced, and momentous
(E) private, beneficial, and minimal

336. Which of the following best captures W. K. Clifford's view about the ethics of belief?

(A) It is always wrong to believe something without sufficient evidence.
(B) It is often beneficial to believe something without sufficient evidence.
(C) It is sometimes wrong to believe something with sufficient evidence.
(D) It is never wrong to believe something with sufficient evidence.
(E) It is usually not beneficial to believe something without sufficient evidence.

337. Questions surrounding the existence of God are typically associated with what major branch of philosophy?

(A) Epistemology
(B) Ethics
(C) Logic
(D) Metaphysics
(E) Aesthetics

338. Aristotle has been interpreted as describing God when he refers to the _____.

(A) unmoved mover
(B) creator of the cosmos
(C) father of Zeus
(D) ground of all being
(E) world spirit

339. The moral theory according to which God is the creator of morality is known as _____.

(A) absolutism
(B) theism
(C) divine command theory
(D) social contract theory
(E) virtue ethics

340. Panentheism is the belief that _____.

(A) God is transcendent but not wholly immanent
(B) God is wholly transcendent and not at all immanent
(C) God is both wholly immanent and transcendent
(D) God is neither wholly immanent nor transcendent
(E) God is sometimes wholly immanent and sometimes transcendent

341. *Natural theology* is best described as _____.

(A) a branch of theology that relies on reason and ordinary experience
(B) a biological theory according to which complexity in nature is best explained by a powerful intelligent designer
(C) the type of theology practiced by pantheists
(D) the type of beliefs we naturally form about God
(E) a form of theology that looks to the natural world as evidence for God

342. *Theodicy* refers to _____.

    (A) the epic Greek poem attributed to Homer

    (B) the study aimed primarily at reconciling God's goodness with the existence of evil in the world

    (C) the belief that human beings can refer to God only by way of what God is *not*

    (D) the study aimed primarily at showing that religious belief is compatible with scientific belief

    (E) theology that proceeds from *a priori* reasoning

343. Theology that proceeds from *a priori* reasoning is known as _____.

    (A) natural theology

    (B) theodicy

    (C) revealed theology

    (D) pantheism

    (E) transcendental theology

The Case for Theism

344. Which of the following is NOT an *a posteriori* argument for the existence of God?

    (A) The cosmological argument

    (B) The teleological argument

    (C) The argument from personal revelation

    (D) The anthropic argument

    (E) The ontological argument

345. "Whatever began to exist has a cause. The universe began to exist. Therefore, the universe had a cause." This argument is a version of what is known as the _____ argument for the existence of God.

    (A) ontological

    (B) cosmological

    (C) teleological

    (D) anthropic

    (E) transcendental

346. What philosopher is traditionally credited with having first propounded the *ontological argument* for the existence of God?

   (A) Plato
   (B) Aristotle
   (C) St. Anselm
   (D) St. Aquinas
   (E) Kant

347. According to "Pascal's wager," _____.

   (A) God cannot create a rock so heavy that He cannot lift it
   (B) in the face of uncertainty concerning God's existence, believing in God is a better "bet" than not believing
   (C) the existence of evil in the world entails that God is either not omnipotent or not omnibenevolent
   (D) God either has reasons for approving of morally good actions or not: if He does, then those reasons are what make those actions good, and not God's approval; if He does not, then God is a capricious being, which contradicts the definition of *God*
   (E) prayer has the power to affect the outcome of games of chance

348. Which of the following claims would not work as a premise in a *teleological argument* for the existence of God?

   (A) A watch must have a watchmaker.
   (B) The human eye is a marvel of bioengineering.
   (C) Nature has a purpose.
   (D) Certain features of living organisms are irreducibly complex.
   (E) Igneous rocks are formed from cooled magma.

349. Which of the following is NOT true of the *ontological argument* for the existence of God?

   (A) It has been criticized by Immanuel Kant for falsely supposing that existence is a property.
   (B) It relies not on empirical data (*a posteriori* evidence) but on reason (*a priori* evidence) alone.
   (C) It relies on the premise that we can conceive of a *greatest possible being*.
   (D) David Hume believed that its premises are tautologically true.
   (E) It has been famously revived in contemporary times by the philosopher Alvin Plantinga.

350. Which of the following is a version of the *moral argument* for the existence of God?

(A) It is immoral not to believe in God. One should not be immoral. Therefore, one should believe in God.

(B) Without the existence of God, morality does not have an objective basis. Morality has an objective basis. So God must exist.

(C) If God did not exist, we would not know right from wrong. We *do* know right from wrong. It follows that God exists.

(D) If God did not exist, we would have no reason to expect punishments and rewards to be handed out fairly. Since we *do* have reason to believe that punishments and rewards will be distributed fairly, there must be a God.

(E) If people believe that morality is created by God, then God must have created morality. Since many people do in fact believe that morality is created by God, God must have created morality. Hence, God must exist.

351. According to some versions of the *argument from reason*, purely naturalistic explanations of the universe _____.

(A) fail because they are self-defeating

(B) succeed because they are scientific

(C) fail because they do not explain supernatural events

(D) succeed because they have a rational basis

(E) fail because there is no reason to believe that the natural world is not illusory

352. The *Kalām argument* is a version of the _____.

(A) cosmological argument

(B) ontological argument

(C) moral argument

(D) argument from reason

(E) argument from personal experience

353. "The universe operates according to natural laws. If there are laws, there must be a lawmaker. Therefore, God exists." This is a version of the _____ for the existence of God.

(A) cosmological argument
(B) anthropic argument
(C) moral argument
(D) argument from reason
(E) teleological argument

354. "The laws of the universe are such that, if any of them were slightly different, mankind could not have existed in the universe." This claim can be used as a supporting premise in which argument for the existence of God?

(A) Cosmological argument
(B) Ontological argument
(C) Anthropic argument
(D) Argument from reason
(E) Argument from personal experience

355. The 13th-century theologian Thomas Aquinas wrote in his famous *Summa Theologica* of the "five ways" in which the existence of God could be demonstrated. Which of the following is NOT one of those arguments?

(A) The argument from contingency
(B) The argument from degree
(C) The argument from morality
(D) The argument from design
(E) The argument from motion

356. One version of the teleological argument for the existence of God is William Paley's argument from design. Which of the following artifacts is mentioned in this argument?

(A) A blueprint
(B) A robot
(C) A watch
(D) A building
(E) A car

357. Physicists have pointed out that several of the basic physical constants described by physics could not have been any different, or a life-sustaining universe would not have existed. How have theists used this insight to argue for the existence of a god?

(A) Physicists are not in a position to claim knowledge about this fact, if their explanation is entirely naturalistic, since there would then be no reason to suppose that our cognitive faculties are truth-tracking.

(B) Since life does exist, the physical constants *must* be what they are, and so speculation is idle.

(C) Since God could have made life exist in any universe, it does not matter which laws of physics govern the universe, because God would exist in any case.

(D) If physical laws exist, there must be a lawmaker. The best candidate for a creator of physical laws is God.

(E) Since it is unlikely that the physical constants should have had, by pure chance, precisely the values needed for a life-sustaining universe, God must have "fine-tuned" the parameters in order to bring about life.

The Case Against Theism

358. The dilemma entailed by the question "Does God have reasons for prohibiting certain actions and recommending others?" is known as _____.

(A) the prisoner's dilemma
(B) Sophie's choice
(C) Pascal's wager
(D) Euthyphro's dilemma
(E) the problem of evil

359. Kant's famous critique of the *ontological argument* for the existence of God argues that _____.

(A) there is no such thing as *a posteriori*, analytic knowledge
(B) existence is not a predicate
(C) God's existence cannot depend on a definition
(D) one could prove the existence of a perfect island with a similar argument
(E) no one has ever seen God

360. Out of the following options, which makes the most sense as a criticism of the *cosmological argument* for the existence of God?

(A) If God created the universe, God must have created evil as well.

(B) There are other, better explanations for the appearance of order in the universe.

(C) Existence is not a predicate.

(D) There is no established, commonly accepted reason to equate "cause of the universe" with a supernatural person.

(E) Religious language should not be understood literally.

361. The 19th-century existentialist philosopher _____ famously has one of the characters in his books exclaim, "God is dead."

(A) Søren Kierkegaard

(B) G. W. F. Hegel

(C) Friedrich Nietzsche

(D) Jean-Paul Sartre

(E) Ludwig Feuerbach

362. Which of the following makes the most sense as a criticism of the *argument from design*?

(A) There have always existed supernatural explanations of mysterious events.

(B) The big bang theory shows that the universe is not infinitely old.

(C) Human beings emerging from matter by chance is just as unlikely as a disassembled Boeing 747 being reassembled by a hurricane.

(D) The theory of evolution by natural selection makes the hypothesis of a supernatural designer unnecessary.

(E) It is illegal to teach creationism in public schools.

363. The *problem of evil* is primarily concerned with the apparent tension between _____.

(A) theism and atheism

(B) natural evil and moral evil

(C) suffering and the existence of God

(D) God's knowledge of our future deeds and free will

(E) the Old Testament concept of God and the New Testament concept of God

364. Some critics of the *teleological argument* for the existence of God have pointed out that _____.

(A) God could have created a different universe altogether
(B) complexity or functionality does not necessarily entail design
(C) the *teleological argument* does not show that God's existence is compatible with suffering
(D) the universe might always have existed
(E) existence is not a property

365. Which of the following is NOT part of a typical criticism of the *cosmological argument* for the existence of God?

(A) The universe might be eternal.
(B) There was no time before the big bang.
(C) The argument does not show us why God should be unique in not requiring a cause.
(D) The universe came into being a finite amount of time ago.
(E) If every object's existence is individually explainable, there is no need to explain the existence of all the objects together.

366. Which of the following makes the most sense as a critical reply to the claim that moral evil is compatible with God's goodness because moral evil is the result of human free will?

(A) Moral evil is not the result of human free will.
(B) God, being omnipotent, could have created a universe in which human beings always freely chose good over evil.
(C) Demons may be responsible for natural evils like earthquakes and tsunamis.
(D) God, being both omnibenevolent and omnipresent, necessarily cancels out all evil.
(E) Natural evil is not the result of human free will.

367. According to the *argument from nonbelief,* _____.

(A) God is unlikely to exist, since many people do not believe God to exist
(B) those who do not believe in God intentionally disbelieve something they know to be true
(C) if atheists do not believe in God, they must not believe in anything
(D) nonbelief in God does not require a justification
(E) if God exists, we would not expect there to be reasonable nonbelievers, and yet reasonable nonbelievers exist

368. The analogy of "Russell's teapot" serves to make the point that
_____.

(A) religious belief is irrational
(B) God could not, logically speaking, make a teapot so heavy that God cannot lift it
(C) the burden of proof is on the theist's side, rather than the atheist's
(D) absence of evidence is not evidence of absence
(E) logical positivism is self-defeating

369. The theistic "free will" response to the problem of evil seeks to reconcile the existence of a benevolent God with _____.

(A) natural evil
(B) causal determinism
(C) moral evil
(D) supernatural evil
(E) psychological determinism

370. Some critics of religion have supported their view by pointing to the suffering and injustices caused in the name of religion. Which of the following is NOT a typical example of a critical response to this type of argument?

(A) What is done in the name of a religion is not necessarily what is taught by that religion.
(B) The worst kinds of evils have historically been perpetrated by atheists like Hitler, Stalin, and Pol Pot.
(C) The fact that bad things can be caused by religious belief does not necessarily entail that religious belief is false.
(D) The existence of suffering and injustice is incompatible with the existence of a benevolent God.
(E) Although suffering and injustice are sometimes caused in the name of religion, many altruistic and beneficent actions are attributed by those responsible for those actions to their religious beliefs.

371. Which of the traditional monotheistic God's attributes is thought by many to be incompatible with free will?

(A) Omnipotence
(B) Omnipresence
(C) Omniscience
(D) Omnibenevolence
(E) Transcendence

Religion and Science

372. The *nonoverlapping magisteria* (or NOMA) view, advocated by Stephen Jay Gould, holds that _____.

(A) the domains of science and religion are different, and so science and religion are not in real conflict

(B) whenever science and religion conflict, science is correct

(C) whenever science and religion conflict, science is incorrect

(D) whenever science and religion agree on something, it is more likely to be true

(E) the domains of science and religion are the same, but each uses a different type of language to describe that domain

373. According to *methodological naturalism,* _____.

(A) there exists nothing apart from what is found in the natural world

(B) the scientific method is necessarily limited to the natural world

(C) human methods of acquiring information are more accurate when they are natural

(D) God created the world at the beginning of time, never to intervene again

(E) certain aspects of the natural world can be explained methodically only with reference to an ultimate creator

374. Prior to the publication of Darwin's *On the Origin of Species*, differences between species tended to be explained in what way?

(A) New species spontaneously come into existence as a result of the position of the stars in the night sky.

(B) Different bacteria, originally from space debris, gave rise to independent lineages of organisms.

(C) Originally, there was only one species. This species was broken into today's many species because of the Biblical "fall from grace" described in Genesis.

(D) Differences between species are what they are because that is how God created them when He created the world.

(E) Differences between species are what they are because differences in environment put different selective pressures on species to evolve in different ways.

375. David Hume's "Of Miracles" presents four arguments against belief in miracles. Which of the following statements is NOT part of any of those arguments?

(A) No miracle has ever been attested to by a sufficient amount of reliable witnesses to merit belief.

(B) The fact that human beings love and delight in wonderful and unexpected stories is a better explanation of our inclination to believe in miracles than that the miracles actually happened.

(C) Belief in miracles occurs more readily in backward, uneducated cultures.

(D) We tend to dismiss miracles alleged to occur in religious contexts other than our own.

(E) The existence of miracles entails the nonexistence of a necessary connection between cause and effect.

376. Four prominent 21st-century naturalist writers have come to be known by the public as "the four horsemen of the apocalypse." Out of the following options, which does NOT list one of those "horsemen"?

(A) Daniel Dennett

(B) Sam Harris

(C) J. L. Mackie

(D) Richard Dawkins

(E) Christopher Hitchens

377. Beliefs or behaviors (such as religious beliefs) that spread from person to person within a culture are called _____.

(A) genes

(B) practices

(C) archetypes

(D) memes

(E) values

378. According to *logical positivism*, supernatural claims are meaningless because _____.

(A) they are intended as expressions of emotional states rather than as claims about external reality

(B) they are merely the beliefs of irrational, superstitious individuals

(C) they have never been proven to be true

(D) they presuppose the existence of a supernatural realm

(E) they are empirically neither verifiable nor falsifiable

379. The scientific approach to gathering knowledge about the world is sometimes criticized for simply *assuming* that nothing supernatural exists. In response, one might point out that this criticism ignores which important distinction?

(A) The distinction between faith and reason
(B) The distinction between methodological naturalism and metaphysical naturalism
(C) The distinction between the supernatural and the metaphysical
(D) The distinction between theism and deism
(E) The distinction between mind and matter

CHAPTER 6

Metaphysics

The Mental and the Physical

380. Which of the following best expresses the core tenet of the theory of *supervenience* (of the mental on the physical)?

(A) A change in mental properties entails a change in physical properties.
(B) The mental and the physical comprise two different fundamental substances.
(C) What we call the physical world is only a mental projection.
(D) All mental properties reduce to physical properties.
(E) Certain mental properties cannot be reduced to physical properties.

381. Which of the following is a common name for the theory that the mental and the physical comprise two different fundamental substances?

(A) Emergentism
(B) Property dualism
(C) Substance dualism
(D) Idealism
(E) Occasionalism

382. The term _____ is often used interchangeably with the term _____.

(A) substance dualism, monism
(B) materialism, idealism
(C) physicalism, property dualism
(D) monism, idealism
(E) materialism, physicalism

383. Most famously defended by Bishop Berkeley in the 18th century, the metaphysical theory of *idealism* declares that _____.

(A) ultimately, human beings are basically good

(B) human brains constantly evolve to achieve greater and greater computational successes

(C) the objects that seem to surround us in space do not have an existence independent of our experience of them

(D) one cannot, without contradiction, doubt one's own existence

(E) philosophical ideas often have the power to significantly alter the flow of history

384. Which of the following is the most accurate name for the metaphysical theory that states that although only physical substance exists, physical objects can have nonphysical as well as physical features or characteristics.

(A) Nonreductionism

(B) Property dualism

(C) Behaviorism

(D) Physicalism

(E) Materialism

385. Which of the following is NOT a likely implication of the *identity* theory of mind?

(A) Experiences are nothing "over and above" physical events.

(B) The relation between brain events and mental events is more than one of mere correlation.

(C) Mental states can be explained in terms of brain states.

(D) The mental and the physical comprise two fundamentally different substances.

(E) There are no mental phenomena that are fundamentally, irreducibly nonphysical.

386. The problem that, according to David Chalmers, has not been sufficiently solved by physicalist theories of mind is known as the "hard problem of consciousness." The *hard problem* is contrasted with the *easy problems*, for which physicalism can account more easily. Which of the following is NOT an example of an *easy problem*?

(A) How is it possible for an organism to discriminate between two different colors?

(B) How is it possible for human beings to report mental states?

(C) Why is there a subjective component to experience?

(D) Why are certain brain states correlated with certain behaviors?

(E) How are we able to remember things that happened in the past?

387. *Qualia* is typically used to refer to which of the following?

(A) The differences between mental states and physical states
(B) The ability to feel pain and pleasure
(C) Publicly accessible expressions of mental states (e.g., wincing or crying when in pain)
(D) The subjective, phenomenal "feel" of experience
(E) The dual properties of the mental and the physical

388. Which of the following gives the most accurate term for any theory that there is just one kind of substance underlying the whole of reality?

(A) Monism
(B) Pantheism
(C) Substance dualism
(D) Epiphenomenalism
(E) Property dualism

389. *Zombies*, in the context of philosophy of mind, are creatures who behave just like us, yet lack conscious experience. The mere possibility of zombies is typically supposed to present a specific problem to _____.

(A) substance dualism
(B) property dualism
(C) monism
(D) physicalism
(E) idealism

390. Which of the following does NOT represent a stance on the causal relation between the mental and the physical in a dualist theory of mind?

(A) Epiphenomenalism
(B) Functionalism
(C) Parallelism
(D) Occasionalism
(E) Interactionism

391. The hugely influential Frank Jackson article "What Mary Didn't Know" includes a thought experiment about a scientist who experiences _____ for the first time in her life.

(A) consciousness
(B) sound
(C) love
(D) color
(E) pain

392. The theory of mind according to which mental states should be thought of in terms of the role they play in the larger system of which they are a part is _____.
   (A) emergentism
   (B) functionalism
   (C) type-type identity theory
   (D) physical reductionism
   (E) property dualism

393. Which of the following claims could NOT be used to criticize substance dualism?
   (A) It is entirely unclear how a nonphysical substance could interact causally with a physical substance.
   (B) The fact that the natural world is "causally closed" entails that the mind cannot affect anything in the natural world.
   (C) Whenever the brain is shut down, the mind shuts down as well.
   (D) If we can explain the natural world without positing immaterial substances (like minds), then Occam's razor requires that we leave immaterial substances out of our explanations.
   (E) It is entirely unclear how subjective properties could emerge out of purely objective properties.

394. The view that mental events have no effect on physical events is known as _____.
   (A) dualism
   (B) occasionalism
   (C) supervenience theory
   (D) functionalism
   (E) epiphenomenalism

395. According to _____, our commonsense beliefs about our own minds are false, and true beliefs about the mind involve only biological or physical explanations.
   (A) substance monism
   (B) eliminative materialism
   (C) functionalism
   (D) epiphenomenalism
   (E) property dualism

Causation and Natural Laws

396. According to the empiricist philosopher David Hume, we never experience a necessary connection between a cause and an effect, only a _____.

(A) weak correlation
(B) *representation* of a necessary cause
(C) contingent connection
(D) constant conjunction
(E) statistical tendency

397. A cowboy is killed by a volley of arrows. Any one of the arrows could have killed the cowboy, but no *one* arrow is the unique cause of the cowboy's death. This scenario exemplifies the phenomenon of _____.

(A) underdetermination
(B) determinism
(C) overdetermination
(D) top-down causation
(E) indeterminacy

398. Which of the following is NOT one of the four types of *cause* identified by Aristotle?

(A) Final cause
(B) Efficient cause
(C) Material cause
(D) Substantial cause
(E) Formal cause

399. Which of the following ideas does NOT at all support the notion of a deterministic universe?

(A) Every event has a cause that is sufficient to bring about that event.
(B) The universe follows natural laws in consistent and predictable ways.
(C) Newtonian physics describes a world in which objects behave in determined ways.
(D) Human behavior cannot be explained by way of sufficient causes.
(E) True randomness cannot exist.

400. Pierre-Simon Laplace theorized in the early 19th century that a sufficiently vast intellect would have the ability to precisely predict future states of the universe on the basis of the present state and the laws of nature. This hypothetical mind has come to be known as _____.

    (A) the evil genius
    (B) Laplace's demon
    (C) Pascal's wager
    (D) the homunculus
    (E) Occam's razor

401. If some event x always brings about another event y, even though other events could bring about y as well, then x is said to be a _____ cause of y.

    (A) necessary
    (B) formal
    (C) necessary and sufficient
    (D) sufficient
    (E) random

402. *Causal conditional* refers to any statement of the form _____.

    (A) absent event x, event y does not happen (as a result of x)
    (B) events x and y overdetermine event z
    (C) event x is correlated with event y
    (D) if event y happens, then it does not happen as a result of event x
    (E) if event x happens, then event y happens (as a result of x)

403. The basic idea behind _____ theories of causation is that statements of cause and effect can best be understood when put in the form "If x had not occurred, y would not have occurred."

    (A) metaphysical
    (B) counterfactual
    (C) Humean
    (D) natural
    (E) antirealist

404. According to *occasionalism*, all events _____.

    (A) actually happen simultaneously
    (B) are caused by God
    (C) have sufficient causes
    (D) have effects
    (E) are predetermined

405. Which of the following is NOT a metaphysical view about the laws of nature?

(A) The universalism view
(B) The antirealist view
(C) The laws-are-necessarily-true view
(D) The antireductionist view
(E) The quantum indeterminacy view

406. Apart from reductionism, what other view does antireductionism about natural laws specifically reject?

(A) Realism
(B) Substance dualism
(C) Supervenience
(D) Universalism
(E) Logical positivism

407. The *deductive-nomological model* of scientific explanation views scientific explanations as _____.

(A) inductive arguments with a sufficient amount of sufficiently strong supporting premises
(B) deductive arguments with at least one premise stating a law of nature
(C) analogical arguments with a repeatedly observed correlation of premises and conclusion
(D) abductive arguments with at least one premise stating a law of nature
(E) inductive arguments with a repeatedly observed correlation of premises and conclusion

408. Which of the following is typically invoked as a scientific counterexample to the notion of a purely deterministic universe?

(A) Einstein's general theory of relativity
(B) Quantum indeterminacy
(C) The big bang theory
(D) Free will
(E) Laplace's demon

409. On one theory of natural laws, the notion of a law of nature should be cashed out in terms of a special relation holding between universals. Which of the following has been a special criticism of this view?

(A) It is not clear what this "special relation" could be.
(B) The existence of universals is not empirically verifiable.
(C) Universals never stand in the relation required for this theory.
(D) Laws of nature do not actually exist.
(E) The theory is true of only some laws of nature.

410. According to David Hume, our concept of causality is derived from the experience of constant conjunctions. How does Immanuel Kant's view about causality differ from Hume's?

(A) Kant's view does not differ from Hume's at all.
(B) According to Kant, our concept of causality is *imposed on*, rather than *derived from*, our experience.
(C) According to Kant, our concept of causality is derived from the experience of strong correlations rather than constant conjunctions.
(D) Kant did not have a view about causality.
(E) According to Kant, our concept of causality is determined by our language.

411. The theory that the identity of a law of nature is determined entirely by matters of fact in the actual universe relies crucially on the notion of _____.

(A) occasionalism
(B) realism
(C) supervenience
(D) determinism
(E) universals

Free Will

412. *Libertarianism*, in the context of metaphysics, is the view that _____.

(A) people have free will, and free will is compatible with determinism
(B) people do not have free will, and indeterminism is false
(C) people have free will, and free will is not compatible with determinism
(D) people do not have free will, but determinism is false
(E) people have free will, and free will is incompatible with indeterminism

413. The view according to which every event is entirely determined and free will is incompatible with determinism is _____.

(A) hard determinism
(B) compatibilism
(C) soft determinism
(D) indeterminism
(E) libertarianism

414. Sometimes *indeterminism* is invoked to defend the possibility of free will. What is the usual critical response to this strategy?

(A) Free will is compatible with determinism, but free will happens to be false.
(B) Indeterminism is false.
(C) *Quantum indeterminacy* refers to an epistemological, rather than metaphysical, phenomenon.
(D) Compatibilism offers a better strategy for defending the possibility of free will.
(E) Indeterminism would make acts of will *random* and, therefore, *out of our control.*

415. According to *compatibilism*, or *soft determinism*, _____.

(A) it could be true that free will exists *and* that everything is determined
(B) it is true that free will exists *and* that everything is determined
(C) it could be true that free will exists *and* that everything is determined, but in fact free will does not exist
(D) it could be true that free will exists *and* that everything is determined, but in fact not everything is determined
(E) it could be true that free will exists *and* that everything is determined, but in fact free will does not exist and not everything is determined

416. So-called *Frankfurt counterexamples* are meant to cast doubt on which of the following?

(A) The absence of constraint
(B) Indeterminism
(C) The principle of alternate possibilities
(D) The avoidability of blame
(E) Self-forming actions

417. According to the *principle of alternate possibilities*, an agent can be morally responsible for an action only if he or she *could have acted otherwise*. This principle has been primarily used to support which of the following claims?

(A) Free will cannot exist, even if indeterminism is true.
(B) Moral responsibility is incompatible with indeterminism.
(C) Not all actions have sufficient causes.
(D) Moral responsibility is incompatible with determinism.
(E) Free will is compatible with determinism.

418. Intuitively, for many intentional, unforced actions, an agent could have chosen to act otherwise than how he or she did. How might a hard determinist best respond to the claim that this intuition supports the existence of free will?

(A) For many actions, an agent could indeed have chosen to act otherwise, but only if conditions prior to the choice had been different.
(B) For many actions, an agent could indeed have chosen to act otherwise, which means that the agent must be morally responsible for those actions.
(C) Intuition supports the existence of free will only if free will is incompatible with determinism.
(D) Intuition supports the existence of free will only if agents are morally responsible for their actions.
(E) For many actions, an agent could indeed have chosen to act otherwise, but only if free will is incompatible with determinism.

419. According to *causal determinism*, _____.

(A) free will does not exist
(B) every event is necessitated by prior events and the laws of nature
(C) every event has a necessary, though not necessarily sufficient, cause
(D) our notion of cause and effect is determined by our experience of constant conjunctions
(E) our notion of cause and effect determines the form of our experience

420. Out of the following, which has seemed to pose the biggest problem for determinism?

(A) The theory of evolution
(B) The existence of luck
(C) Quantum physics
(D) Our inability to predict the future
(E) God's foreknowledge of the future

421. Which of the following is NOT an explicit position on the issue of free will?

(A) Compatibilism
(B) Causal determinism
(C) Hard determinism
(D) Libertarianism
(E) Incompatibilism

422. Which of the following best describes the relation between *libertarianism, soft determinism*, and *hard determinism*?

(A) They are all compatible with one another.
(B) Libertarianism is compatible with soft determinism, but not with hard determinism.
(C) Soft determinism and hard determinism are compatible with one another, but not with libertarianism.
(D) Soft determinism and hard determinism are both compatible with libertarianism, but not with one another.
(E) They are all incompatible with one another.

423. Which of the following makes the least sense as a criticism of hard determinism?

(A) If free will does not exist, then people are never morally responsible for their actions.
(B) Free will is not incompatible with causal determinism.
(C) Hard determinism maintains that our actions are not caused by prior events.
(D) Quantum physics tells us that there is indeterminacy in the universe.
(E) Hard determinism does not explain the phenomenological fact that my actions often seem as though they are "up to me."

424. Suppose I longed for a bottle of whiskey, but I also wished that I didn't have that longing. This scenario would best illustrate the notion of
_____.

(A) a self-forming action
(B) free will
(C) a second-order desire
(D) fatalism
(E) moral responsibility

425. Which of the following is probably the main motivation for subscribing to *soft determinism* (or *compatibilism*)?

(A) The theory allows one consistently to hold two intuitively attractive views—that we have free will and that determinism is true.

(B) The theory makes the most sense out of our ordinary practice of holding one another morally accountable for actions.

(C) The theory best explains the way in which human beings typically come to make choices.

(D) The theory makes no claim about whether there is a contradiction between free will and determinism.

(E) The theory best explains the phenomenological fact that my actions often seem as though they are "up to me."

426. One of the most influential statements on free will can be found in the writings of David Hume. According to Hume, morally free and responsible actions _____.

(A) never occur

(B) are those actions that are caused by an agent

(C) entail indeterminism

(D) are incompatible with determinism

(E) are uncaused

Identity and Modality

427. The principle that no two distinct objects can have all properties in common is known as _____.

(A) the bundle theory

(B) Leibniz's law

(C) the principle of sufficient reason

(D) Occam's razor

(E) supervenience

428. Which of the following best describes the field of *mereology*?

(A) The study of ultimate reality

(B) The study of the relation between consciousness and the objects of consciousness

(C) The study of the relations between parts and other parts and between parts and their wholes

(D) The study of what makes a person a person

(E) The study of the criteria of identity

429. The "ship of Theseus" thought experiment presents several interesting problems. Which of the following is NOT a subject for any of those problems?

(A) Material constitution
(B) Identity over time
(C) Part-to-whole relations
(D) Temporal parts
(E) Personal identity

430. The idea that *x* and *y* might be the same *f* and yet not the same *g* is typically cited as evidence for _____.

(A) partial identity
(B) absolute identity
(C) cross-world identity
(D) relative identity
(E) vague identity

431. Two (or more) things can be *more or less* identical with each other in virtue of shared properties. But a thing can be *completely* identical only with itself. These two claims illustrate the distinction between _____.

(A) perdurance and endurance
(B) quantitative identity and qualitative identity
(C) personal identity and material constitution
(D) part and whole
(E) eternalism and temporalism

432. Identity is typically thought of as an *equivalence relation*. The equivalence relation is _____.

(A) asymmetric, coreflexive, and transitive
(B) symmetric, reflexive, and transitive
(C) symmetric, reflexive, and euclidian
(D) asymmetric, reflexive, and total
(E) symmetric, reflexive, and total

433. The morning star and the evening star are both identical with Venus, and yet the following could be true: "Sam believes the morning star is Venus, but he does not believe the evening star is Venus." This fact casts doubt on which principle?

(A) The anthropic principle
(B) The principle of sufficient reason
(C) The principle of the identity of indiscernibles (Leibniz's law)
(D) The uncertainty principle
(E) The principle of substitutivity

434. A *rigid designator* is any term that denotes _____.

(A) identity between an object and itself
(B) the same object over time
(C) logical constants
(D) the same object in every possible world
(E) inflexible logical principles

435. The three basic alethic *modal* properties are _____.

(A) reflexivity, transitivity, and symmetry
(B) simplicity, complexity, and chaos
(C) necessity, possibility, and impossibility
(D) dualism, materialism, and idealism
(E) certainty, doubt, and ignorance

436. *Modal realism* is the theory that _____.

(A) the real world necessarily exists
(B) possible worlds are real
(C) only necessary beings are real
(D) reality is just one of several modes of possibility
(E) only contingent beings are real

437. _____ modality is directly about objects in the world, while _____ modality is about statements.

(A) Absolute, relative
(B) *De re, de dicto*
(C) Necessary, contingent
(D) *A priori, a posteriori*
(E) Analytic, synthetic

438. Which of the following claims presents the greatest difficulty for *perdurantist* theories of personal identity?

(A) A person is best thought of as extending not only in space but in time as well.

(B) The whole is sometimes greater than its parts.

(C) Parthood is a supervenient property.

(D) Intuitively, a person is wholly, not just partially, present at any moment of his or her existence.

(E) Since any person could have had a life quite different from what he or she in fact had, a person can have *transworld identity*.

439. *Mereological essentialism* is the view that _____.

(A) logical tautologies are necessarily true

(B) wholes have their parts essentially

(C) a person is best thought of as extending not only in space but in time as well

(D) a person's essence is determined by his or her material constitution

(E) a whole can have essential properties that its parts do not have individually

440. Saul Kripke's influential text *Naming and Necessity* includes a careful analysis distinguishing between the related, but oft-conflated, notions of _____.

(A) idealism, monism, and phenomenalism

(B) objective truth and subjective truth

(C) transitivity, reflexivity, and symmetry

(D) absolute truth and relative truth

(E) *a priori* truth, necessary truth, and analytic truth

441. Leibniz's law (the identity of indiscernibles) has been criticized on the basis of a thought experiment wherein one imagines a perfectly symmetrical universe containing only two equally sized symmetrical spheres. Why is this criticism typically rejected?

(A) Leibniz's law is a logical truth, so it could not possibly have empirically based counterexamples.

(B) The spheres have different properties, since they differ both in spatial location and in material constitution.

(C) A perfectly symmetrical universe is a logical impossibility.

(D) The spheres would be indiscernible.

(E) A universe containing only two symmetrical spheres would not be symmetrical.

CHAPTER 7

Epistemology

The Nature of Knowledge

442. Derived from the Greek words for *knowledge* and *study*, _____ is that area of philosophy concerned with the nature and scope of knowledge.

    (A) metaphysics
    (B) ontology
    (C) epistemology
    (D) rationalism
    (E) empiricism

443. According to the classic definition, *knowledge* refers to _____.

    (A) true belief held with conviction
    (B) certainty
    (C) justified true belief
    (D) a state of enlightenment
    (E) objectively true belief

444. Epistemology primarily focuses on *propositional* knowledge (knowing *that* such and such is the case). Propositional knowledge is typically contrasted with what other types of knowledge?

    (A) Practical knowledge and knowledge by acquaintance
    (B) Artistic knowledge and moral knowledge
    (C) Moral knowledge and practical knowledge
    (D) Artificial knowledge and knowledge by acquaintance
    (E) Knowledge by acquaintance and knowledge by description

445. Suppose I suddenly believed, for no particular reason, that I will win the lottery tomorrow, and suppose I actually end up winning. Most philosophers would say that I didn't *know* that I would win, since my true belief lacked _____.

(A) certainty
(B) conviction
(C) content
(D) justification
(E) predictive success

446. According to *foundationalist* analyses of knowledge, _____.

(A) beliefs can be justified on the basis of basic, self-evident beliefs
(B) the foundation of all knowledge is justification
(C) beliefs are justified according to how well they fit in with a person's overall set of beliefs
(D) knowledge is the primary basis for all human behavior
(E) beliefs can be justified on the basis of an infinite regress of justified beliefs

447. Which of the following has presented the biggest challenge to the classic analysis of knowledge as justified true belief?

(A) Academic skepticism
(B) Gettier cases
(C) Empiricism
(D) Frankfurt counterexamples
(E) Rationalism

448. Which of the following names the theory according to which knowledge is true belief arrived at by a trustworthy process?

(A) Coherentism
(B) Contextualism
(C) Reliabilism
(D) Foundationalism
(E) Internalism

449. The debate between *internalists* and *externalists*, in the context of epistemology, is primarily about _____.

(A) whether or not knowledge is even possible

(B) whether or not everything necessary to provide justification for a belief must be immediately available to the believer's consciousness

(C) whether or not what makes a belief true must be something that is immediately available to the believer's consciousness

(D) whether the objects of belief are inside the mind or in the external world

(E) whether or not we can ever know the contents of another person's mind

450. Which of the following claims best describes the central thesis of *coherentism*?

(A) Beliefs are justified according to how well they fit in with a person's overall set of beliefs.

(B) Knowledge requires not mere evidence, but also *warrant*.

(C) Beliefs are not justified unless they are internally consistent.

(D) Knowledge requires not mere true belief, but also *justification*.

(E) Beliefs are justified if they are arrived at by a trustworthy process.

451. Who wrote the important 1969 essay "Epistemology Naturalized"?

(A) Bertrand Russell

(B) Alvin Plantinga

(C) W. V. O. Quine

(D) Philip Kitcher

(E) Edmund Gettier

452. Arguably, one of the first analyses of knowledge as justified true belief can be found in _____.

(A) Plato's *Dialogues*

(B) St. Augustine's *Confessions*

(C) Descartes's *Meditations*

(D) Hume's *Enquiry Concerning Human Understanding*

(E) Wittgenstein's *Tractatus Logico-Philosophicus*

453. Which of the following epistemological theories is least likely to disagree with reliabilism?

(A) Evidentialism
(B) Externalism
(C) Coherentism
(D) Internalism
(E) Foundationalism

454. Why does the *correspondence theory of truth* pose a special problem for coherentism?

(A) It entails that coherentism does not respond adequately to the regress problem.
(B) A system of beliefs may be internally consistent despite those beliefs not corresponding to reality.
(C) Everything necessary to provide justification for a belief must be immediately available to the believer's consciousness.
(D) It entails that coherentism does not provide an adequate solution to skepticism.
(E) Justification is mostly a matter of providing evidence for a belief, but coherentism does not require that one have evidence for a justified belief.

455. Which of the following could be an example of a *Gettier case*?

(A) I have the experience of waking up in my own bed. Unbeknownst to me, I am actually sleeping in a hotel room and only *dreamt* that I woke up.
(B) I point at what appears to be a zebra, and I say, "I know that's a zebra." It turns out it was actually just a cleverly disguised mule.
(C) I conclude, as I often do, from the empty food bowl that my cat has come in for the night. My cat has indeed come in for the night, but, unbeknownst to me, a neighbor cat actually snuck in and ate the cat food before my cat got a chance to eat anything.
(D) Today is Friday. Usually the bank is open on Saturday, but since it is very important that I get my check into my bank account before Monday, I don't want to take the chance that it won't be open, so I deposit the check today.
(E) I experience my life as though nothing is out of the ordinary. I experience growing up, getting a job, getting married, and so on. In reality, I am just a brain in a vat, hooked up to a giant computer that creates a virtual reality indistinguishable from ordinary reality.

456. Which of the following is a main tenet of *virtue epistemology*?

(A) Having knowledge is a prerequisite for being virtuous.

(B) Epistemic value and evaluation primarily concern agents and communities.

(C) Justification of belief is mostly a matter of having evidence directly available.

(D) Epistemic value and evaluation primarily concern beliefs or sets of beliefs.

(E) Knowledge ought to be valued more highly than mere true belief.

The Objects of Knowledge

457. Some statements are said to be known to be true not because there is empirical evidence for them, but because they are *analytically* true. Which of the following is NOT a statement that can be known in this way?

(A) All bachelors are males.

(B) Triangles have three sides.

(C) If Socrates is a man, and all men are mortal, then Socrates is mortal.

(D) If it rains today, and if Socrates has an umbrella, then Socrates will take an umbrella with him today.

(E) Green is a color.

458. Which of the following best names the thesis that knowledge is primarily arrived at through the senses?

(A) Rationalism

(B) Epistemology

(C) Metaphysics

(D) Internalism

(E) Empiricism

459. *A priori* statements are _____.

(A) statements that are true in virtue of meaning

(B) statements that can be known to be true without having to consult experience

(C) statements that are true only subjectively

(D) statements that can be known to be true by consulting experience

(E) statements that are true in all possible worlds

460. According to Plato, the only true objects of knowledge are _____.

  (A) sense-data
  (B) the eternal Forms
  (C) mathematical truths
  (D) ideas in the mind of God
  (E) empirical facts

461. Which of the following would not be an object of knowledge by acquaintance?

  (A) The streets of Amsterdam
  (B) Hillary Clinton's dermatologist
  (C) It is time to go
  (D) Vintage bicycle serial numbers
  (E) What time it is

462. Propositions that are known to be true only in some possible worlds are _____.

  (A) synthetic truths
  (B) *a priori* truths
  (C) contingent truths
  (D) necessary truths
  (E) *a posteriori* truths

463. According to Descartes, potential objects of knowledge are known to be true when they are _____ and _____.

  (A) analytic, *a priori*
  (B) corporeal, concrete
  (C) *a priori*, necessary
  (D) *a posteriori*, synthetic
  (E) clear, distinct

464. Which of the following claims about *a posteriori* knowledge is the most accurate?

  (A) *A posteriori* knowledge is derived from the senses.
  (B) *A posteriori* knowledge concerns only contingent truths.
  (C) *A posteriori* knowledge is derived from pure thought or intuition.
  (D) *A posteriori* knowledge concerns only synthetic truths.
  (E) *A posteriori* knowledge concerns only analytic truths.

465. Which of the following claims is most accurate as a description of *idealism?*

(A) Certain features of our experience of the physical, external world are actually created by our own minds.

(B) Truths about the physical world are ultimately just truths about perceptions or experiences.

(C) In order for a statement to be meaningful, it must be verifiable by experience.

(D) Truths about the physical world are truths about a mind-independent, external existence.

(E) We can know the contents of our own minds much better than we can know what is in the physical, external world.

466. According to _____, we can know truths about the world simply by using reason and intuition.

(A) logic

(B) empiricism

(C) rationalism

(D) antirealism

(E) idealism

467. "2 + 2 = 4" has been at various times argued to be an example of all but which of the following?

(A) An analytic truth

(B) An *a posteriori* truth

(C) An *a priori* truth

(D) A synthetic truth

(E) A necessary truth

468. Which of the following best describes Immanuel Kant's view on our knowledge of space and time?

(A) Our knowledge of space and time is *a posteriori.*

(B) We do not have knowledge of space and time because space and time do not really exist.

(C) Our knowledge of space and time is *a priori.*

(D) We do not have knowledge of space and time because those categories are beyond the realm of human understanding.

(E) Our knowledge of space and time is contingent.

469. Saul Kripke's *Naming and Necessity* questions the notion that there are
no truths that are both necessary and *a posteriori*. Which of the following
statements does Kripke use to make his point?

(A) Hesperus is Phosphorus.
(B) $2 + 2 = 4$.
(C) All vixens are foxes.
(D) Water is H_2O.
(E) What goes up must come down.

470. According to Plato, the eternal Forms can be compared to what is seen
in clear daylight, while ordinary sense-perceptions can be compared
to _____.

(A) hallucinations caused by too much heat
(B) what is seen under a magnifying glass
(C) shadows cast on the wall of a dimly lit cave
(D) what is seen under pale moonlight
(E) what is heard as a faint echo across a valley

471. _____ concerns the challenging claim that the contents of any
mind but one's own can never constitute objects of knowledge.

(A) Psychological egoism
(B) Idealism
(C) Pyrrhonian skepticism
(D) Contextualism
(E) The problem of other minds

472. According to Immanuel Kant, whatever human beings can have knowledge
about resides in the *phenomenal* world, whereas the _____ world,
the world of things-in-themselves, is forever beyond our cognitive grasp.

(A) noumenal
(B) real
(C) supernatural
(D) objective
(E) virtual

The Limits of Knowledge

473. Which of the following is the best critical response to the claim that one can tell that one is not dreaming by citing some experience that distinguishes dreams from waking reality?

(A) This is not something we need to worry about, practically speaking.
(B) A benevolent God would not allow us to be so incapable of telling the difference between dreams and waking reality in the first place.
(C) Any distinguishing experience could itself be dreamt.
(D) Waking reality is sometimes very dreamlike.
(E) There is no difference between dreams and waking reality.

474. René Descartes, in his *Meditations on First Philosophy*, considers several skeptical scenarios. The contemplation of what possibility allows Descartes to cast doubt even on mathematical knowledge?

(A) The possibility that he is just a brain in a vat
(B) The possibility that he is insane
(C) The possibility that an evil demon is deceiving him
(D) The possibility that he is dreaming
(E) The possibility that he is in the Matrix

475. Which of the following best illustrates the *epistemic closure principle*?

(A) If p entails q, and if p is true, then q is true.
(B) If I don't know that I'm not just a brain in a vat, then I don't know that I have hands.
(C) If p entails *not-q*, then if I know that q is true, I know that p is false.
(D) If I know that I have hands, then I know that I'm not just a brain in a vat.
(E) If I know that p is true, and if I know that p entails q, then I know that q is true.

476. The *argument from analogy* is an attempt to defuse skepticism about _____.

(A) the external world
(B) abstract objects
(C) God
(D) other minds
(E) mathematical truth

477. An empiricist would most likely be skeptical about the existence of _____.

(A) *a posteriori* knowledge
(B) objective knowledge
(C) *a priori* knowledge
(D) fallible knowledge
(E) subjective knowledge

478. G. E. Moore, early 20th-century defender of common sense, attacked skepticism about the external world with these famous words:

(A) "Doubt makes sense only in a context of non-doubt."
(B) (Uttered while kicking a rock) "I refute it thus!"
(C) "God's perfect benevolence would not allow me to be so deceived in belief that the external world exists."
(D) "Here is one hand, and here is another."
(E) "If it can be sprayed, it's real."

479. The kind of skepticism displayed in Descartes's works is best described as _____.

(A) scientific skepticism
(B) ordinary skepticism
(C) methodological skepticism
(D) Pyrrhonian skepticism
(E) academic skepticism

480. David Hume is famous for raising skeptical doubts about all but which of the following?

(A) Causality
(B) The self
(C) The external world
(D) Miracles
(E) Mathematics

481. According to Hilary Putnam's famous article "Brains in a Vat," if you experienced your life exactly as you normally would, but you were actually a brain in a vat, _____.

(A) you would not be able to tell that you were a brain in a vat
(B) you would not be able to truthfully say, "I know that I am not a brain in a vat"
(C) you would not be able to tell that you were not a brain in a vat, even if you weren't a brain in a vat
(D) you would not be able to truthfully say, "I am a brain in a vat"
(E) you would be able to tell that you were a brain in a vat

482. "If I know that I have hands and that having hands entails that I am not just a brain in a vat, then I know I am not a brain in a vat. I don't know that I am not just a brain in a vat. Therefore, I don't know that I have hands." This skeptical argument relies on which of the following principles?

(A) The principle of sufficient reason
(B) The closure principle
(C) The principle of alternate possibilities
(D) The anthropic principle
(E) The principle of substitutivity

483. Pyrrhonian skepticism involves _____.

(A) denying that we know anything
(B) withholding assent from any nonevident claim
(C) denying that we know anything about the external world
(D) knowing that we know nothing
(E) methodological suspension of judgment until certainty is reached

484. Throughout the years, philosophers have suggested a variety of skeptical scenarios. Which of the following is NOT considered a standard scenario for raising the possibility of skepticism?

(A) The scenario wherein one is just a brain in a vat
(B) The scenario wherein one is dreaming
(C) The scenario wherein one is living in a Matrix-style virtual reality
(D) The scenario wherein one is merely a character in another person's dream
(E) The scenario wherein one is being deceived by a powerful demon

485. The claim that true belief never rises to the level of knowledge because it is always possible to doubt the belief presumes _____.

(A) the infallibility of knowledge
(B) that knowledge is subjective
(C) the fallibility of knowledge
(D) that doubt is always rational
(E) the factivity of knowledge claims

486. According to Descartes, what is the one thing that I can know with absolute certainty?

(A) I have a brain.
(B) God exists.
(C) I exist.
(D) The external world exists.
(E) 2 + 2 = 4.

487. According to David Lewis, in most ordinary contexts we can properly ignore skeptical scenarios, and so ordinary knowledge claims are often true, despite the possibility of skeptical scenarios. The rule that licenses this "proper ignoring" is the rule of _____.

(A) propriety
(B) nonassent
(C) attention
(D) common sense
(E) ignorance

The Semantics of Knowledge

488. According to *epistemic contextualism*, the _____ of a knowledge claim partially depends on the context in which the knowledge claim is uttered.

(A) assertability
(B) usefulness
(C) meaning
(D) possibility
(E) believability

489. *Semantic theories* of knowledge are concerned with _____.
- (A) the metaphysics of knowledge
- (B) the usefulness of knowledge
- (C) the scope and limits of knowledge
- (D) the meaning of the word *know*
- (E) the phenomenology of knowledge

490. According to some *ordinary language philosophers*, such as Norman Malcolm and Ludwig Wittgenstein, the meaning of the word *know* may change depending on the particular use to which the word is put in different situations. This claim can be seen as an early precursor to which of the following views?
- (A) Relativism
- (B) Coherentism
- (C) Contextualism
- (D) Externalism
- (E) Subject-sensitive invariantism

491. *Subject-sensitive invariantism* disagrees with *epistemic contextualism* on all but which of the following points?
- (A) Whether the truth of knowledge claims depends partially on how high the "stakes" are
- (B) Whether it is the *extension* of a knowledge claim or the *content* of a knowledge claim that is determined by context
- (C) Whether *know* always means the same thing or its meaning changes depending on context
- (D) Whether it is the context of the *subject* of a knowledge claim or the context of the *attributor* of a knowledge claim that determines the standard of justification
- (E) Whether what is required for *knowledge itself* may change depending on context or is independent of context

492. Which of the following claims has been used most often to discredit *epistemic contextualism*?
- (A) The contextualist confuses *warranted assertability* conditions with *truth conditions*.
- (B) The contextualist has no way to respond to skepticism.
- (C) The contextualist cannot point to any other words that are context sensitive.
- (D) The contextualist assumes that knowledge is even possible.
- (E) The contextualist has no account of *how* context affects meaning.

493. A major strength of *epistemic contextualism* is often thought to consist of its potential to provide a satisfying solution to _____.

(A) the problem of other minds
(B) the problem of evil
(C) philosophical skepticism
(D) the problem of vagueness
(E) questions concerning personal identity

494. According to _____, statements of the form "*s* knows that *p*" are actually short for statements of the form "*s* knows that *p* rather than *q*."

(A) relativism
(B) indexical contextualism
(C) subject-sensitive invariantism
(D) contrastivism
(E) internalism

495. Suppose I tell you, "It's cold in here!" in order to get you to shut an open window. The difference between the literal content, *it is cold in here*, and the implied content, *I would like you to shut the window*, marks the distinction between _____.

(A) semantics and pragmatics
(B) internalism and externalism
(C) contextualism and invariantism
(D) indexical contextualism and nonindexical contextualism
(E) assertability and truth

496. *Invariantism*, in the context of the semantics of knowledge, is the denial of which of the following theories?

(A) Relativism
(B) Externalism
(C) Reliabilism
(D) Contextualism
(E) Internalism

497. Which of the following best describes a *relativist* model for the semantics of *know*?

  (A) Statements of the form "*s* knows that *p*" do not have a fixed meaning, but change their meaning relative to contexts of utterance.
  (B) All knowledge is relative.
  (C) Statements of the form "*s* knows that *p*" are short for statements of the form "*s* knows that *p* relative to standard φ."
  (D) The extension of statements of the form "*s* knows that *p*" is fixed relative to the context of utterance.
  (E) Statements of the form "*s* knows that *p*" are not true or false *simpliciter*, but true or false *relative* to a contextually determined standard of justification.

498. Which of the following makes the most sense as a contextualist critique of subject-sensitive invariantism?

  (A) Our intuitions about ordinary language support the thesis that the standard of justification is sensitive to the context of the *attributor* of a knowledge claim rather than to the context of the *subject* of a knowledge claim.
  (B) Subject-sensitive invariantism does not provide a solution to the problem of other minds.
  (C) Our intuitions about ordinary language support the thesis that statements of the form "*s* knows that *p*" are not true or false absolutely, but true or false only relative to a contextually fixed standard of justification.
  (D) Subject-sensitive invariantism does not explain how context affects the truth value of knowledge claims.
  (E) Our intuitions about ordinary language support the thesis that statements of the form "*s* knows that *p*" are actually short for statements of the form "*s* knows that *p* rather than *q*."

499. According to some epistemic contextualists, the word *know* functions like an *indexical*. Which of the following words is not an example of an indexical?

  (A) Here
  (B) I
  (C) Meaning
  (D) Tomorrow
  (E) That

500. Which of the following constitutes the main challenge for *invariantist* models for the semantics of *know*?

(A) Accounting for the intuitions about ordinary language cases that seem to show that there are different senses of the word *know*

(B) Showing that the word *know* does indeed function like an indexical

(C) Accounting for the intuitions about ordinary language cases that seem to show that there is only one sense of the word *know*

(D) Showing how an invariantist treatment of the semantics of *know* can respond to skepticism in a satisfying way

(E) Accounting for the intuitions about ordinary language cases that seem to show that most knowledge claims are just false

ANSWERS

Chapter 1: Philosophy and Reasoning

1. (E) This is an ethical question, which cannot be settled by observation or experiment. It belongs to the province of ethics, which is a philosophical discipline. The rest of the choices are questions that can be addressed by observation or experiment.

2. (B) Free will is a philosophical question that cannot be settled by observation or experimentation. Arguments must be made to see how best to philosophically settle the matter.

3. (A) The optimal minimum wage is an economic question, in and of itself. There may be ethical considerations that go into how economic conditions should be determined for the sake of low-wage earners, but determining the optimal minimum wage in service of this goal is an economic question.

4. (D) Philosophical questions can be asked by anyone at any time. Philosophy may also cost nothing, but this is not what makes it universally applicable. Usually an education helps in pursuing philosophy.

5. (D) Philosophers make use of principles to form arguments, and to do this they have to make sure they remain consistent to those principles wherever they apply. The point of appealing to principles is to find generally applicable reasons for a conclusion rather than just arguing for conclusions on whatever basis one wants.

6. (C) Being committed to a principle in a certain case means being committed to applying it wherever it is applicable. It would be contradictory to accept a principle but only apply it in restricted cases.

7. (A) Questions of justice are ethical questions. The other choices are empirical questions that can be settled by the natural or social sciences.

8. (E) Analyses of the nature of knowledge itself and its conditions are the province of epistemology. Empirical questions of how learning happens or why people are interested in various topics are psychological questions.

9. (B) Metaphysics has to do with the nature of reality independently of how we may think about it. Questions about people's beliefs or empirical questions about how many of a certain kind exist are not philosophical.

10. (D) Normative ethics deals in general principles that govern what makes right actions right and is not restricted to particular issues. The nature of ethical facts or moral knowledge has to do with metaethics, which deals in the nature of moral reality.

11. (E) Applied ethics deals with specific ethical issues. Questions of right conduct come from normative ethics, which applies to specific issues, but applied ethics is restricted to specific topics one at a time.

12. (C) Value theory is the discipline within ethical theory that deals with questions of what is most important overall and to be valued in life. It is not directly concerned with what makes right conduct right, although right conduct may be at least part of what is to be valued.

13. (A) Metaethics is the discipline within ethical theory that deals with the nature of moral reality and moral facts. The moral facts would be what are referred to when making moral judgments, but the rightness of moral judgments is a separate issue.

14. (A) The moral justifiability of a particular kind of action is an area dealt with by applied ethics. The question of what makes actions right or wrong in general is dealt with by normative ethics. (E) is an empirical question; given an answer to it, there would still be further question whether the death penalty is justifiable.

15. (D) Questions of justice as applied to punishment in a particular situation are dealt with by applied ethics. (A) is a biological question whose answer still leaves ethical questions open, (B) is a psychological question, (C) has to do with what is economically prudent for oneself, and (E) is a sociological question.

16. (A) What is worth motivating a person is a question of value theory. (B) is a socio-economic question and still leaves open what is to be valued in life. (C) is a specific issue and would be addressed by applied ethics. (D) is a question of economic value, not ethical value. (E) would be best addressed by metaethics.

17. (B) Whether it could be ethical to break a promise is a general question of normative ethics. (A) and (C) are psychological questions, (D) is an empirical question, and (E) is a question of political philosophy.

18. (E) Whether duty always obligates is a question of normative ethics. (A) and (D) are psychological questions, (B) is a legal question, and (C) is a historical question.

19. (B) The in-principle resolvability of moral disagreements is a question of meta-ethics, having to do with the nature of moral facts. (A), (C), and (E) are empirical questions. (D) is a question that would be best addressed by normative ethics, since it attempts to address the ethically right answer in a particular type of situation.

20. (D) The nature of moral disagreements is the province of metaethics since moral disagreements would have to do with moral facts. (A) and (B) are questions of psychology, and (C) and (E) are questions of applied ethics.

21. (E) Logic expresses necessary connections between statements and thus tells which truths must follow from which. It does not tell which statements are true or give answers by itself.

22. (E) An argument's logic tells whether the truth of the conclusion is validly deducible from the truth of the premise. This is the specific meaning of *logic* in philosophy, not the common meaning given by (A) or (C).

23. (A) Logic describes the forms of inference that are valid, from which one makes arguments. Individual statements may be true or false independently of particular structures of inference.

24. (D) A conditional is an "if . . . then . . ." statement, so it expresses a relation of consequence between the truth of its antecedent (what comes after *if*) and the truth of its consequent (what comes after *then*).

25. (D) If a conditional is true, then it is true that its antecedent, if true, entails the truth of its consequent.

26. (E) If a conditional is true, then it is not possible for its antecedent to be true while its consequent is false. If this is possible, then the conditional must be false.

27. (C) If a conditional is true, then its consequent *follows from* its antecedent—that is, if the antecedent is true, the truth of the consequent must follow.

28. (D) A conditional is false just when its consequent might be false while its antecedent is true—thus, a counterexample to a conditional shows a conditional to be false.

29. (D) An argument is itself a conditional—an "if-then" statement—so its premises collectively correspond to the antecedent of a conditional: the statements that, if true, would ensure the truth of the conclusion (consequent).

30. (E) An argument must contain a general principle that ties specific statements together and ensures a certain conditional truth.

31. (B) The principles of an inductive argument cannot prove a conclusion—it would not be logically inconsistent to suppose the premises true but the conclusion false—but they can show how the conclusion is probable.

32. (D) A valid argument is one for which the truth of the premises would entail the truth of the conclusion, so an invalid argument is one for which the premises might be true but fail to entail the conclusion.

33. (C) This is an inference in the form of *modus tollens*, which is valid because a true conditional is one for which its antecedent cannot be true while its consequent is false.

34. (A) Although the premises and the conclusion of this argument are true, the premises themselves do not ensure the truth of its conclusion, so the argument is invalid. An argument cannot be sound without first being valid.

35. (E) Although the first premise of the argument is false, if the premises were both true they would entail the conclusion, so the argument is valid.

36. (C) The premises of this argument entail the truth of the conclusion, so the argument is valid. Since the premises are also true, the argument is also sound.

37. (E) The argument is valid because it is a valid instance of *modus tollens*: proceeding from the negation of the consequent to the negation of the antecedent. One of the premises (the first one) is false, however, so the argument is not sound.

38. (C) This argument's premises validly entail their conclusion, being a valid instance of *modus tollens*. The premises are true, so the argument is also sound.

39. (A) A logical fallacy consists of an invalid inference—it does not necessarily mean its conclusion is false, but that its premises fail to entail the conclusion.

40. (C) This is an instance of the fallacy of denying the antecedent, since for all the argument says, it could still be that if you don't go to school you pass your exam for some other reason.

41. (B) This argument is a valid use of *modus tollens* in its logic; however, it is unusual to draw a logical conclusion with a premise like the second one, which is why it sounds unusual. If the premises were true, however, the conclusion would have to logically follow.

42. (C) Even though ordinarily it might be presumed true that "if we don't like the movie, we won't recommend it to others," that goes beyond what the argument itself says: "If we like the movie, we'll recommend it to others" does *not* in itself entail that "if we don't like the movie, we won't recommend it to others."

43. (D) This is an instance of the fallacy of affirming the consequent: "they" could have saved money for some other reason than taking the bus.

44. (A) This argument is a valid use of *modus tollens*; what is wrong with it is that the conditional connects two things that are actually unrelated. In terms of pure validity of form, however, the argument is a valid one: *if* the premises were true, the conclusion would logically follow.

45. (D) This argument invalidly attempts to reason by affirming the consequent and proceeding to a true antecedent, which does not necessarily follow: if "you are rich now" is true, this may well be true for some other reason than that "you must have made a lot of money in the stock market."

46. (B) This is a valid argument, since *if* the first premise (the conditional) were true, then since "I am not a gorilla" is true, it would logically follow that seven is not a prime number. Of course, the problem with the argument is that the first premise is obviously false, but this does not detract from the argument's validity.

47. (A) This is a valid argument, proceeding from the truth of the antecedent to the truth of the consequent.

Chapter 2: Ethical Theory

48. (D) Realism states that there are objectively correct facts. (A) is not sufficient to establish this. (B) and (C) are based on mistaken ideas about the meaning of *realism*. (E) is not entailed by realism since it could be that people use emotions in moral judgment while the moral facts are objective.

49. (A) If the moral facts are objective, then it could be that everyone is morally wrong: if morality were subjective, then this could not be correct since in that case people would ordinarily be morally correct according to their own subjective standards.

50. (B) The objectivity of moral truths is definitive of ethical realism. Ethical realism does not mean most people judge objectively or even believe that moral truths are objectively correct.

51. (C) If there were objective moral facts, one might well expect people to agree on what they are, but since people typically do not, this is a difficulty for ethical realism. (A) is what one would expect if moral truths were objective, and (B) is what one would expect for moral facts.

52. (E) Our intuitions about our most strongly held moral judgments are that they are objectively true; otherwise, we would presumably not hold such judgments at all.

53. (B) Antirealism about a set of facts says that they are what they are ultimately because we say so. (A) opposes this. (C) is very likely to be realist rather than antirealist, and (D) and (E) do not entail that morality is dependent on people's judgments about it.

54. (A) If the moral facts are independent of our judgments, then they are objectively the way they are, and our judgments are right only if they are right about how the facts objectively are. (B) and (C) oppose this view, and (D) and (E) do not entail it.

55. (D) Most of our moral judgments are such that we tend to think they are objectively correct, but antirealism says that moral judgments are never objectively correct.

56. (C) Natural law ethics says that moral facts are derivable from natural facts, which are objective, and therefore moral facts would also have to be objective.

57. (B) Subjectivism says that morality is subjective rather than objective, and this is inconsistent with realism. (A) is not inconsistent with realism since it could be objectively true that moral facts are relative to the observer.

58. (E) If the moral facts are objective, then people can be objectively wrong about their morality. If (A), (B), (C), or (D) were false, this would not entail the falsity of ethical realism.

59. (C) Realism entails that correctness would have to be objective correctness. (A) is not entailed by realism, since it could be objectively true that ethical facts can change, as in some forms of relativism. Likewise, the falsity of (B), (D), and (E) would not entail the falsity of realism.

60. (B) Ethical antirealism itself only entails the falsity of ethical realism. (A) is entailed not by ethical antirealism, but by antirealism about all of the facts, moral or otherwise: one could be an ethical antirealist without being an antirealist about all of the facts. Rather than requiring that anyone might be wrong about morality, antirealism says that everyone might be automatically right about morality, if it is subjective. (E) is an antirealist view, but antirealism by itself does not entail it.

61. (D) Ethical antirealism denies ethical realism, which is (D). Ethical realism is compatible with the view that there are moral facts, just maintaining that they are subjectively determined.

62. (A) A challenge to realism is the diversity of moral views, which makes it seem more as if morality is subjective, which involves ethical antirealism. This does not prove that morality is truly subjective, however. This also does not mean that people are willing to change their own moral views.

63. (B) People's ethical views are typically held unqualifiedly, without the thought that they are relative. Believing the moral facts upon which one's judgments are based to be objective requires a realist interpretation of moral facts.

64. (D) Ethical relativism may involve other views such as (C) or (E), but the view itself says that ethical facts are relative to some frame of reference or other. It does not say that there are no ethical facts, or that ethical facts vary with the situation.

65. (B) The main motivation for ethical relativism is to account for the fact that there is a diversity of ethical views, which is what would be expected if ethical facts varied according to the perspective of the observer. It may involve reducing conflict or taking subjectivity into account, but these are not the main underpinnings for the view itself.

66. (C) Individually based ethical relativism says that moral correctness can only be defined according to each individual. It does not require that individuals do or do not change their moral views.

67. (B) A *norm* in the ethical sense is a moral standard, however that is determined. (A) does not amount to a norm, since something merely accepted by a culture may not amount to an ethical norm. (C) and (D) are based on common, statistical use of the term *norm*, which differs from its ethical sense.

68. (C) Cultural ethical relativism says that each culture determines its own set of ethical norms, so moral norms can only be judged within a culture to see if they conform with that culture's norms. According to cultural relativism, different cultures may be expected to have different norms, so these cannot be judged between cultures.

69. (E) Since a cultural relativist must say that ethical norms can only be judged within a culture insofar as they may vary from the norms of that culture, cultural relativism must say that each culture is free to determine its own moral norms. A cultural relativist need not say that different cultures *have* to differ in their norms, nor that morality is a matter of taste.

70. (C) It would be inconsistent with both individual and cultural relativism to hold that moral facts could apply equally to everyone (unless it were held that humankind formed a single culture, which would make it not really relativist). (E) is a consequence of individual ethical relativism, but not part of the view itself. It is also not a consequence of cultural ethical relativism.

71. (D) Cultural relativism says that norms that are maintained by a different culture cannot be judged outside of that culture. This is a weakness insofar as there may be practices that are permissible according to the norms of another culture that seem objectively wrong, yet from outside the perspective of that culture, cultural relativism says that they cannot be judged.

72. (A) Both individual and cultural relativism have to maintain that whatever an individual or culture, respectively, determines as its moral norms, it cannot be judged outside of that individual or culture. This means that individuals or cultures, respectively, cannot be judged objectively wrong in the ethical norms that they determine for themselves. This seems incorrect since it would certainly seem possible for there to be moral norms that are morally wrong.

73. (A) Ethical absolutism says that ethical norms hold within an absolute frame of reference and are not relative to individual or culture. This is a straightforward denial of any form of ethical relativism. Realism is not inconsistent with relativism, since it could be objectively true that moral norms are relative to individual or culture. Traditionalism is not inconsistent with relativism, since it could be that moral norms are derived from each culture's traditions.

74. (B) If an individual's own norms provide the only standard by which moral judgment can be made, then each individual is in effect morally infallible in his or her judgments, since it would be possible to morally err only by going against one's own moral norms.

75. (E) If a culture's own norms provide the only standard by which moral judgment can be made, then each culture is in effect morally infallible, because it is possible to morally err only in terms of whatever moral norms are in effect in a given culture.

76. (C) For cultural ethical relativism to be true, one must be able to definitively say where one culture ends and another begins so that it is clear where one can and cannot apply a culture's ethical norms. But definitions of culture are not so precise and make it difficult to draw such boundaries. (D) simply states a consequence of cultural relativism.

77. (A) It seems possible for cultures or individuals to morally progress, in becoming more ethically correct over time. But since ethical relativism entails that each individual or culture is automatically infallible in the norms that it already has, it would mean that what we would think of as progress is merely arbitrary change from one moral standard to another. For example, a culture may once have tolerated slavery and then abolish it; according to relativism, this is a mere change, not an objective improvement.

78. (C) Having moral norms that apply to everyone is not compatible with norms being relative to culture or person. If there is widespread agreement or disagreement, or diversity in the moral norms that people believe in, this would be compatible with either relativism or absolutism.

79. (D) Psychological relativism is an empirical view describing the way in which people believe in moral norms. It does not entail ethical relativism—that moral norms really are relative to the observer—nor that people ought to have varying moral beliefs.

80. (A) Psychological relativism says that people's beliefs are often shaped by forces relative to their standpoint. It does not entail anything about what should be the case, what moral norms there actually are, or what norms are relative to.

81. (E) Consequentialism is an ethical theory that explains what is right or wrong about actions entirely in terms of their consequences. If consequences of an action are harmful to someone, the action is judged as morally bad. If consequences of an action are beneficial to someone, the action is judged as morally good.

82. (A) Many of the actions judged bad by commonsense morality are harmful—for example, stealing, killing, abusing—and consequentialism explains this in terms of the harm itself as a consequence of such actions. Thus, it is an explanatory benefit of consequentialism if it gives many of the same answers as we would expect of an ethical theory. The rest of the answer choices are not typically characteristic of consequentialist ethical theories.

83. (D) Supererogatory acts go "above and beyond" what is required. They are good but not obligatory. That is, it would not be morally objectionable not to do an act that is considered supererogatory. This is in contrast with an action that is obligatory, which is both morally good and such that it would be bad not to do it.

84. (E) Consequentialism says that all morally good acts are those that have good effects, and vice versa. This does not seem to allow it to draw a sharp distinction between acts that are good and obligatory on the one hand, and acts that are good but not obligatory—supererogatory acts—on the other. While (B), (C), and (D) are true, and (A) may be true of some forms of consequentialism, they are not the reasons why consequentialism has difficulty accounting for supererogatory acts.

85. (B) Consequentialism rates actions as morally good or bad based only on their consequences, so according to that theory, whether an action is done with good or bad intentions does not make a difference in and of itself as to whether the action is morally good or bad. Consequentialism can assign moral responsibility insofar as it can recognize who is responsible for actions with good or bad consequences.

86. (D) It is not characteristic of consequentialism itself that other people's good cannot be taken into account: its main variant, utilitarianism, takes the general good into account. Since consequentialism places a moral value only on the goodness or badness of the consequences of individual actions, it cannot find value in justice, intentions, or moral value as considered apart from actions.

87. (E) It is not possible to have rules that everyone will agree upon or that always give the best results without exception. Unlike act consequentialism, rule consequentialism says that there should be morally binding rules such that if they are followed, the results are better than they would otherwise have been.

88. (A) Both act utilitarianism and rule utilitarianism share the disadvantages that consequentialism has. Rule utilitarianism would support some of the same traditional rules of morality as maximizing utility. As a form of utilitarianism, rule utilitarianism has the disadvantage that in some individual cases, rule following may fail to maximize utility.

89. (D) *Utility* denotes a material sense of *happiness*, in which beings are able to flourish as much as possible. (A) and (B) are not things that utility easily takes account of, and (C) and (E) are based on a misunderstanding of the ethical term *utility*, which differs from other uses of the word.

90. (C) Utilitarianism is a major variant of consequentialism, because utilitarianism seeks to bring about the consequences of maximizing utility (i.e., happiness) for the greatest number. (D) is another variant of consequentialism, and (B) and (E) are opposed to utilitarianism (and consequentialism).

91. (C) Utilitarianism is essentially impartial because it is concerned with maximizing utility for the greatest number of beings that are capable of experiencing utility, no matter who or what they are. It is true that it is consequential, but that is not a general advantage unless one is already a consequentialist.

92. (C) Instrumental value is that which is valued only because of its bringing something else about. Utilitarianism places moral value on good intentions only insofar as they successfully bring about an increase in utility. It places intrinsic value on (good) consequences and is normally understood to include pleasure as a form of utility.

93. (D) This action fails to maximize utility since a hungry person is lacking in utility. Utilitarianism would not consider it wrong to make a promise, but only to keep it at the expense of maximizing utility. Rule breaking is not only permissible but also required by utilitarianism in cases where it maximizes utility. All other things being equal, (B) would be an action that maximizes utility and thus would be morally right according to utilitarianism.

94. (B) Stealing is permissible, and perhaps even obligatory, according to utilitarianism when it is done toward the goal of maximizing utility. The other answer choices all describe cases in which harm is done without increasing utility overall, which is what utilitarianism considers morally wrong.

95. (C) The 19th-century British philosopher John Stuart Mill, after Jeremy Bentham, was a major proponent of utilitarianism in the Western philosophical tradition. He wrote an influential short work entitled *Utilitarianism*. Smart was a 20th-century utilitarian.

96. (B) Ethical egoism is an ethical theory stating what should be the case. It understands the moral good in terms of people's unique ability to act according to their own interests. (A) is an empirical claim about what is psychologically the case about people. An ethical egoist is not committed to (C), which does not necessarily conflict with (B). (D) is relativism, which is not what ethical egoism aims at, although it is possibly entailed by some theories of ethical egoism.

97. (A) Nietzsche firmly contended that one should act according to one's own interests, and that those who are most capable of furthering their own interests should in fact do so at the expense of others. He criticized traditional morality as "master and slave morality."

98. (D) The key premise in Rand's argument is that each person's ultimate value is himself or herself. Conjoined with the idea that each person is best at looking after his or her own interests, this is supposed to entail that each person should only do things that further his or her interests. (A) and (B) are not premises in the argument, and (C) and (E) are ideas that Rand argues for, but not premises themselves.

99. (E) Ethical egoism must maintain that it is wrong to do something that does not further one's own interests, because the energy that is used to do so could have been used to further one's own interests, which is the ultimate value for each person. Neglecting the ultimate value is considered immoral by almost any ethical theory, so this is what ethical egoism is ultimately premised upon. (A) does not necessarily conflict with ethical egoism's central claim. (B) is incorrect because everyone could be an ethical egoist, according to ethical egoism. (C) is incorrect because almost certainly different things will be valuable to people. (D) is possible according to ethical egoism, but not necessarily so.

100. (B) Helping others at the expense of furthering one's own interests is what ethical egoism is fundamentally opposed to. The other answer choices are all compatible with ethical egoism as long as doing so furthers one's own interests.

101. (C) Ethical egoism maintains that whatever is in one's own interests is what one should do. (A) is not part of ethical egoism, and (B) is false because sometimes the desires of others will help advance your interests. (E) is part of psychological egoism, but not ethical egoism.

102. (B) Ethical egoism maintains that people should only further their own self-interest, because each person is the best at doing that for him- or herself. Therefore, trying to help others only keeps them from doing what they are best at doing for themselves. (A) is not required by ethical egoism since ethical egoism says what should be the case, not what is the case. (C) is not a primary motivation for ethical realism, and (D) and (E) are not centrally relevant to ethical egoism.

103. (A) In putting each person's self-interest first, ethical egoism goes strongly against most traditional ethical ideas, which tend to include as a central feature that one should do right to others. Ethical egoism not only does not require one to do right to others but also forbids it in cases when doing so goes against, or even fails to advance, one's own interests. (B) is false because ethical egoism does take account of each person's right to act in favor of his or her interests. (C) is false because the value of each person's own interests is determined according to ethical egoism.

104. (B) Ethical egoism is consequentialist because it accounts for the good in terms of bringing about one's own interests, which is a consequence of certain actions. (A) requires the interests of everyone to be furthered rather than each person just looking after his or her own. (C), (D), and (E) would strongly conflict with ethical egoism.

105. (D) Psychological egoism claims that as a matter of psychological fact, when people do whatever they want, they will only do what is in their own interests. It does not claim that this should be the case; it just says it is the case. It does not claim that people find traditional morality too difficult, because people may be constrained to follow traditional morality.

106. (C) Psychological egoism says that people are only capable of acting in their own self-interests. If this is the case, then people will never really act in ways that do not in some manner advance their self-interest. It does not entail (A) because people could be constrained by psychological egoism yet not believe that that is what should be the case. It does not entail (B) because people could still help others if it also serves their own self-interest. (D) is not a question that would be settled by the truth or falsity of psychological egoism. (E) is a fundamental misunderstanding of the term.

107. (E) If psychological egoism is true, then ethical theories that expect people to act in ways that are not in their own interests cannot be true. This is because of the commonly accepted principle "ought implies can"—if it is true that one ought to do something, it is presumed that one is able to do that thing. Psychological egoism does not imply anything about what ethical theories people believe in, since people might believe in any sort of ethical theory while psychological egoism is true.

108. (C) Genuine self-sacrifice would constitute a counterexample to psychological egoism, which has to maintain that people only want to do what is in their own self-interest, not sacrifice their interests for the sake of others. Psychological egoism would therefore have to say that even in cases of self-sacrifice leading to death, people think they are furthering their interests in some way.

109. (A) Plato's *Republic* contains a fable about a ring of invisibility as a "thought experiment" to find out what people would do if they could get away with anything. The story is supposed to show that people would break laws and social conventions if they could in order to get whatever they want. The story does not suggest anything about whether this should be the case.

110. (B) The "ring of invisibility" thought experiment from Plato's *Republic* is meant to show that if people could get away with anything they want to do, they would ruthlessly further their own interests. This would mean that in ordinary circumstances, the only reason that people do not do so is that they are constrained by the fear of repercussions. According to psychological egoism, people will not act in accordance with traditional morality if given the choice to further their own interests. If psychological egoism is true, then people will act in accordance with their own interests whether they believe in psychological egoism or not.

111. (B) Psychological egoism must maintain that genuine altruism—people acting in other people's interest without thought of gain for themselves—is impossible. But it seems that genuine altruism is possible, so this weighs against psychological egoism. (A) is false since psychological egoism is motivated by the fact that people do tend to primarily further their own self-interest. (C) is false because psychological egoism does not entail anything about what should be the case, but rather concerns what is the case about human nature. (D) is false because psychological egoism does not entail ethical egoism as a normative truth. (E) is false because no one in particular stands to gain from the truth or falsity of psychological egoism.

112. (E) According to Kant's moral theory, the good will is the epicenter of all moral good. Actions are thus to be judged according to the intentions with which they were done. Even actions that have good results have no moral content, according to Kant, unless they are done in accordance with a specific will to do good.

113. (C) Kant thought that the good will involved a sort of duty that is done for its own sake. According to Kant, moral goodness is the easiest to identify when it is done purely for the sake of doing what one is obligated by the moral law to do. (A) and (D) may be virtues, but they have moral value, for Kant, only insofar as they are practiced with an overriding will to do the good.

114. (D) Kant explains the good in terms of doing what is rational. According to Kant's view, moral failures can always be explained as some form of irrationality. Thus, if one always does what is rational, then one will avoid doing moral wrong. The pursuit of goodness always leads one toward greater rationality.

115. (D) According to Kant's theory of rationality, an act is only rational if the reason for which it was done could be satisfied if everyone acted in the same way toward the same ends. Some actions that reach their goals could not be thus reached if everyone acted that way, so making an exception of oneself by acting in such a way is contrary to reason, according to Kant.

116. (B) The categorical imperative can be stated in various forms, but it always states what must be done no matter the circumstances in order to maintain rationality and thus uphold one's moral duty. For example, "Never treat people as means to an end," because if one did this, it would imply that it is acceptable to be treated as a means to an end oneself, and this conflicts with one's identity as a rational agent in the first place, which all people are by definition.

117. (C) A hypothetical imperative says that "*if* you want to achieve the goal *x*, you should do *y*." A categorical imperative, on the other hand, states simply that "you should always do *x* (no matter what)."

118. (A) A categorical imperative does not simply state what is good, but states what should always be the case, including actions that are forbidden. It does not include an "if" clause, which would make it a hypothetical imperative. The categorical imperative, for Kant, states what is necessary in order to maintain standards of rational action and therefore not deviate from moral goodness.

119. (A) A *maxim* of an action is the reason for which it was done. The role of a maxim in a hypothetical or categorical imperative is the reason that an action is done. A categorical imperative is such that the maxim can be universalized, which according to Kant's theory makes the action morally right.

120. (B) Divine command theory says that *given* that God exists, then moral obligation comes from the need to obey God's commands. It is not a way of demonstrating that God exists, and its truth would not entail that there could be no moral obligation without God's existence.

121. (E) Divine command theory only asserts that God's will determines what is morally right and therefore obligatory. God could exist without divine command theory being true. (B), (C), or (D) might be true or false independently of the truth or falsity of divine command theory.

122. (D) In *Euthyphro*, Socrates is trying to get Euthyphro to tell him what piety is, apart from its being what pleases the gods. Socrates does not call into question his piety, or the particulars of the case that Euthyphro is involved in. Socrates and Euthyphro are each defendants in a court case for unrelated matters.

123. (C) Euthyphro maintains that piety is that which pleases the gods. According to this attempted definition, piety is not ultimately measured in terms of people or justice or what one can get out of being pious.

124. (C) Socrates grants that what is pious must be that which pleases the gods, but he rejects this as a definition since it still leaves the question open of what pleases the gods, besides something's being pious. Socrates wants to know what quality an action must have in order to please the gods and therefore be pious.

125. (B) What is known as the "Euthyphro dilemma" arises from the question of what is pious, or moral. Although in the *Euthyphro* dialogue the question was about the definition of piety, the point generalizes to divine command theory about morality itself. If something is made good by the fact that God commands it, then either God commands it because it is good, in which case God's commanding it is not what makes it good, or whatever God commands, even if it was evil, would be automatically good.

126. (B) Aristotle associated both virtue and the good with finding a mean between extremes. It is easy to find extremes, but it takes experience and cultivation to locate an appropriate mean. Likewise, Aristotle thought that the experience that it takes to cultivate virtue is well suited to making good choices. It is not just a matter of exerting enough effort. (A) is true in a sense but does not answer the question. (D) would be true according to consequentialism.

127. (D) Aristotle thought that virtue is essentially a property of persons, as moral agents, and thus whatever is morally good is that which a virtuous person would do. (C) is true of virtue but not definitive of it. (B) may be a part of virtue but is also not definitive of it.

128. (E) Theories that define the morally good in terms of the virtuous typically hold that virtue is not something that everyone has or even is capable of, but rather is something that comes with seasoning, care, and experience. (C) is backward; virtue theory would say that good actions come naturally to a virtuous person. (A) is hedonism.

129. (A) A problem for virtue ethics is the issue of defining good actions in and of themselves. One might want a definition of good actions that does not require mention of virtue, since a virtuous person is just supposed to be one who would act with moral rightness. The issue of whether morality or virtue is supposed to come first is sometimes called the "priority problem."

130. (C) Divine command theory defines goodness in terms of what God commands. Virtue ethics defines goodness in terms of what a virtuous person would do. Both of these theories have as a weakness that goodness is defined in terms of a certain type of entity, which could lead to a circular account according to which moral goodness is what a certain type of person would or will do, and a certain type of person is how morality is defined.

131. (B) Value theory is the philosophical subdiscipline that seeks to understand what basic things we value, or should value. This involves distinguishing between things that are pursued for their own sake and things that are pursued for the sake of other things.

132. (C) The overall set of values that explains our life values includes things that are pursued for their own sake and things that are pursued for the sake of other things. In either case, value theory seeks to discern what the reason is for valuing what we value.

133. (B) An instrumental good is an "instrument" that is used to get something else. Therefore, it is valued not for its own sake, but only for what it can bring about. Instrumental goods must eventually lead to things that are valued for their own sake. (D) is not necessarily the case because pleasure need not be the intrinsic good that instrumental goods help bring about.

134. (E) Things that are valued intrinsically are valued for their own sake—they are good not because of what they can bring about, but because they are valuable just for being what they are. Intrinsically good things can be valued for a variety of reasons, but they must be valued according to what they are in and of themselves.

135. (D) Many things are valued instrumentally—that is, for something else that they can bring about. Instrumental good may be pursued for the sake of other instrumental goods, but ultimately all instrumental goods must lead to something that is valued for its own sake. Therefore, it will be the basis of an explanation for everything that we do.

136. (C) Value theory is most like a fundamental theory of everything because it seeks to understand that which is ultimately valued, which in turn explains what everything else we value is good for. It is not necessarily the actual appreciation of good things, but rather understanding what is valued and why.

137. (A) Aristotle thought that there must be things that we value intrinsically, because instrumentally valued things must be valued for the sake of something else. Since instrumental values must eventually lead to something, that something must be where the chain of instrumental values ends, and that can only be something that is intrinsically valued.

138. (D) Aristotle thought that every rational person will have his or her various pursuits organized and oriented toward something that explains them all, which is the single ultimate value that one orients one's life toward. This need not take the form of (E), and (C) is incorrect because a variety of interests may not be all oriented toward a specific intrinsic good.

139. (D) Aristotle argued that there must not only be things that are valued intrinsically, but that there must be one thing intrinsically valued that everything else in one's life points toward. He argued that this must be so because otherwise we would have no rational basis for choosing between pursuing various goods or understanding what is valued for what reasons.

140. (D) Value theory is the philosophical discipline whose purpose is to discern what people value that explains their actions and pursuits, to determine what goods are intrinsic and which are pursued for the sake of other things, and to determine what sorts of things *should* be valued. (E) is part of the process of determining what is ultimately valued but is not the ultimate goal of value theory.

141. (B) *Eudaimonia* is a Greek term for ultimate goodness in life that is sometimes translated as *happiness*, but this can be misleading because many people today associate happiness with certain subjective experiences. *Eudaimonia* is defined not in terms of feelings, however, but in terms of well-being in an objective sense, which may or may not be associated with feelings.

142. (A) Stoicism held that "happiness" is attained when one is in accordance with virtue, whatever else that entails. This means that it might bring pleasure, or might even bring pain. This is why to be *stoic* today means to endure hardships impassively. To be a Stoic in the original sense meant not necessarily embracing hardship, nor thinking that pleasure is bad, but that what is morally best is independent of either.

143. (A) *Hedonism* means valuing whatever brings about the most pleasure. This could be sensory pleasures, but not necessarily. A person who considered contemplation the highest pleasure and pursued that above all else and for that reason would be a hedonist, in philosophical terms. The important thing about hedonism is that it is measured in subjective terms of experiences of well-being.

144. (C) The experience-machine thought experiment of Robert Nozick is to imagine that one is hooked up to a machine that simulates all the positive experiences one could want, so that they would seem indistinguishable from real experiences. Thus, any subjective state of well-being can be generated not by real experiences, but by a machine that cuts one off from the real world by doing so.

145. (E) The experience-machine thought experiment is supposed to draw one's attention to a strong intuition that most of us have. This intuition says that although the subjective experience of having experiences simulated by a machine would be the same as real experiences of such a kind, this would not be nearly as worthwhile as real experiences. The thought experiment is thus meant to show us that we are already committed to a principle that says that subjective states of well-being cannot be what is ultimately valued.

146. (B) If the good of virtue comes from its tendency to bring about pleasure, then that would mean that virtue is an instrumental good and pleasure the intrinsic good that it brings, which indicates hedonism. (A) would indicate that deprivation of pleasure is not the ultimate evil, which means that something besides pleasure is valuable. (C) would be agreed upon by anyone who engages in value theory. (E) is compatible with hedonism or nonhedonism, depending on whether subjective states of well-being are the ultimate value or not.

147. (D) A hedonist, in philosophical terms, is one who maintains that subjective experiences of pleasure or well-being, however they may come about, are what is ultimately valuable in life. (E) would be agreed upon by both the hedonist and nonhedonist, but they would disagree on what constitutes "happiness."

148. (C) A hedonist is committed to the view that the ultimate good is pleasure, or more broadly, subjective well-being. This means that such is therefore the only real intrinsic good. Other things that may bring it about, including virtue, if it does bring about pleasure, would therefore be instrumental in value for bringing about something else that is intrinsically good.

149. (B) If virtue is valuable above all else, this would entail the falsity of hedonism, since not only would virtue not necessarily bring pleasure, but also it is something other than pleasure. (A) and (E) could be things that bring about pleasure, so they would not necessarily be alternative to hedonism.

150. (E) If we can be harmed in other ways than by being deprived of pleasure, this entails that pleasure is not the ultimate good: if it were, then being deprived of pleasure would be the only thing that could ultimately harm us, or bring about moral badness. (A) is a controversial claim, although arguably a challenge to hedonism. (B) is compatible with pleasure's being the ultimate good, as long as some kind of it leads to true "happiness." (C) comes from the perspective of hedonism itself. (D) would be agreed upon by anyone who pursues value theory, whether hedonist or not.

Chapter 3: Applied Ethics

151. (A) Various justifications may be given for the death penalty in order to defend it, but the primary motivation for having it in the first place is as a way for justice to be done on the worst of crimes, in order for the law to officially recognize them as the worst possible and requiring the ultimate penalty in order for justice to be done.

152. (B) The death penalty is not necessarily the result of criminals not getting a fair hearing, so the requirement that those accused of crimes be treated fairly in court is not a criticism of the death penalty. If the death penalty is just, then it will in fact be a result of guilty defendants who deserve it getting a fair hearing in court.

153. (A) The defense of capital punishment that says that it is needed in order to deter violent crime is motivated not by justice, but by preventing crime in the first place.

154. (D) One objection to capital punishment says that it is inconsistent to carry it out in order to condemn murderers, because if the taking of life is an ultimate moral evil, then taking life to punish murder is self-contradictory by defeating its own motivation.

155. (B) The hypocrisy objection to capital punishment assumes that all taking of life is murder, whereas it is not necessarily inconsistent to punish unjust taking of life (murder) by a taking of life, if capital punishment is itself a just punishment for murder. If the hypocrisy objection were accepted, then other types of punishment would have to be condemned as well just for their taking away something valuable from the person being punished.

156. (C) One objection to capital punishment says that we should not exercise the death penalty at all because of the risk of executing the innocent. But this does not address the main motivation for the death penalty, which is that it is needed in order to carry out justice for the most serious crimes. A more direct criticism of the death penalty would address the central motivation for the death penalty itself and show that it is actually unjust even when those who receive it are guilty.

157. (D) One justification for capital punishment says that it should be carried out in order to provide an example and deter further crime. This justification is not concerned with justice, so whether or not capital punishment is justified against those who receive it is not directly relevant to the deterrence justification.

158. (B) The justice-driven motivation for capital punishment is itself just concerned with redressing wrongs—that is, recognizing that some crimes such as murder violate the ultimate value—by giving the ultimate punishment for those crimes. (D) is one particular version of this motivation, but not all justice-related motivations for capital punishment need be concerned with proportional justice.

159. (C) If criminals are punished because it is believed that this will improve them, then this is a motivation based on a specific outcome, and not on the need for retributive justice. (A), (B), and (E) would have to do with punishing according to the severity of the crime, which would mean that it is concerned with retributive justice. (D) would also be concerned with carrying out justice.

160. (B) Consequentialism is the ethical theory that says that the moral good of an action is determined by its consequences. The justification for the death penalty that says that what is good about it is that it is a deterrent to crime is concerned with justifying the death penalty because of its positive consequences. It is therefore an instance of consequentialism in its moral reasoning.

161. (A) Objections to capital punishment that claim it is unjust focus on the punishment itself and who receives it, and claim that it is not fitting. (A) assumes that what would make capital punishment morally justifiable is whether it works as a deterrent to crime, so it is not based on a principle of justice.

162. (E) The defense of capital punishment that claims it is needed in order for equal justice to be served supposes that in general, the punishment for a crime should be the same thing as the crime itself. But this cannot serve as a practical and just general principle on which to decide what punishments to mete out for which crimes in all cases. Crimes such as embezzlement, prostitution, and kidnapping are examples for which equal justice—doing the same thing to criminals that they did—would be impossible.

163. (D) Proportional justice requires that worse crimes be given worse punishments than less bad crimes. This does not require that punishments be equal to the crimes themselves, but it does require that there be a scale of punishments of different severities such that the punishments are aligned with crimes of different severities.

164. (E) Proportional justice requires that the worst crime be given the worst punishment out of the punishments that are given for crimes. It does not require that capital punishment is actually the worst punishment that is given. A less severe punishment could be the worst punishment that is given on a sliding scale of justice. Capital punishment *could* be compatible with proportional justice, but it is not required by it.

165. (B) Justice-driven motivations for capital punishment usually cluster around the idea that capital punishment is required in order to recognize the severity of the crime. The idea that criminals should be made an example of, on the other hand, is motivated by the view that capital punishment should deter crime by making criminals specially avoid the kinds of crimes that result in the death penalty.

166. (A) Proponents of capital punishment are typically concerned with carrying out justice, so establishing that it is not necessary for justice to be served is the single point that is usually sufficient to establish in order to undermine the central motivation for it. (B) and (D) may be sufficient to argue against capital punishment but are not necessary to do so.

167. (C) Equal justice means that people who commit immoral acts deserve to have the same thing happen to them. It thus would require that criminals be punished by having the same crimes they commit visited upon them.

168. (A) Capital punishment today, when it is used, is used as a way to punish the most serious crimes. It once was a common punishment, but most developed countries today have discontinued using it. Most philosophers argue against it, on several bases, including that it is not required in order for justice to be done. The U.S. Constitution rules out "cruel and unusual punishment" but does not require, or inveigh against, the death penalty.

169. (D). (A), (B), and (E) provide limited bases on which to argue against capital punishment. (C) is an objection that cannot gain traction unless it were shown that capital punishment itself is an instance of murder, but the wrongness of capital punishment is the issue to be established, and so the contention that it is hypocritical cannot be based on that supposition. The most likely motivation for capital punishment is that equal retribution be done on murderers in order for justice to be done, so the most effective basis in general for arguing against capital punishment will be to show that equal retribution is a generally unworkable system of justice.

170. (B) The terms refer to the two main practical approaches to animal ethics. Each of these two approaches can be seen as consequences of the two main theoretical approaches to animal ethics: the *animal rights* position and the *animal welfare* position. The animal rights position maintains that animal ownership needs to be abolished (hence the term *abolitionism*), while the animal welfare position maintains that animals ought to be protected from undue or unnecessary harm (hence the term *protectionism*).

171. (B) Animal rights proponents do not claim that animals have rights not had by humans (such as the right to behave in any manner whatsoever, or the right not to be killed under any circumstance). Nor do they suppose that animals are on entirely equal moral footing with humans. Rather, the animal rights proponent tends to claim only that animals have at least one right in common with human beings: the right not to be treated as property.

172. (C) While animal rights proponents and animal welfare proponents are both concerned with the well-being of animals, animal welfarists do not agree with the animal rights position that animals have the right not to be used as property. Rather, the animal welfare position encourages humane and responsible animal stewardship, which typically involves treating animals like property.

173. (A) Positions in animal ethics are most typically supported by either appealing to the moral imperative to maximize well-being (a *consequentialist* approach to ethics) or appealing to a moral duty to respect a being's rights (a *deontological* approach to ethics). (B), (C), and (D) involve other philosophical approaches to ethics that are not as frequently appealed to in debates surrounding animal ethics.

174. (C) While many books concerning animal ethics have been written in recent decades, it is commonly accepted that Peter Singer's work *Animal Liberation* is the book most influential in launching the contemporary animal rights movement.

175. (A) While animal rights proponents and animal welfare proponents are both concerned with the well-being of animals, animal welfarists do maintain that animals may be used as property. Since animal rights proponents maintain that animals ought never to be used as property, they cannot agree entirely with the animal welfare position.

176. (A) A popular defense of the idea that animals cannot be bearers of moral rights is that human beings have traits not had by animals, such as rationality and autonomy. This argument relies on the premise that only those beings who have rationality and autonomy can be bearers of moral rights. The case of the brain-damaged infant provides a counterexample to this claim, as most people believe that even brain-damaged infants have some moral rights.

177. (A) *Behaviorism* is a methodological approach to psychology that focuses on directly measurable effects on behavior by directly measurable external stimuli. Intervening mental states are not regarded by behaviorists as being explanatorily relevant, and so behaviorism is often seen as encouraging a purely mechanistic view of human and animal psychology alike.

178. (E) *Animal welfarism* is the view that, while animals may be treated as property, their well-being ought to be maximized as much as practically possible. Hence, there are two main ways of disagreeing with the view: First, one could deny that animals feel pain at all, and so their well-being need not concern us. Second, one could deny that animals may be treated as property.

179. (E) René Descartes is famous for his metaphysical doctrine of *dualism*, according to which human beings have both a physical body and a nonphysical mind. Descartes is often described as holding the view that dualism is not true of nonhuman animals, who are limited to purely physical being.

180. (B) *Animal rights* proponents often criticize *animal welfarism*'s position of responsible animal ownership for hindering progress in the improvement of the human treatment of animals. Animal welfare proponents have countered that the animal rights view that animal ownership should be abandoned altogether is unlikely to gain public traction, and that animal welfarism presents a much more attractive and feasible option for society at large.

181. (D). (A), (B), (C), and (E) do not address the claim that causing animals unnecessary pain is wrong only because treating animals cruelly might cause us to treat human beings cruelly as well. (D), on the other hand, presents a clear counterexample to the claim, as the intuition cited there contradicts the very premise of the claim.

182. (A) *Deontological* approaches to ethics in general focus on moral *duties*. Hence, according to deontological approaches to animal ethics, how animals ought to be treated depends on what our duties are toward them.

183. (A) A popular defense of the idea that animals cannot be bearers of moral rights is that human beings have traits not had by animals, such as rationality and autonomy. This argument relies on the premise that only those beings who have rationality and autonomy can be bearers of moral rights. The case of the brain-damaged infant provides a counterexample to this claim, as most people believe that even brain-damaged infants have some moral rights.

184. (D) According to Tom Regan, the primary property necessary for being a bearer of moral rights is *having a life that matters to the being that has it*. Regan's term for beings who have this trait is *subject-of-a-life*.

185. (D) Typically, definitions of *terrorism* describe terrorism as involving harm inflicted on *civilians*, not enemy combatants.

186. (C) People tend not to publicly condone the practice of terrorism. Many, however, will forgive or pardon the practice in certain cases.

187. (B) This claim in no way clashes with the information given in the original claim. The claim merely points out a distinction actually made in the original claim.

188. (D) Consequentialism is the ethical theory according to which only the consequences of an action determine the moral status of the action.

189. (A) Deontological theories of ethics make the related notions of *rights* and *duties* central to their theoretical frameworks.

190. (C) *Jus in bello* means, literally, "justice in war."

191. (A) Just War theorists believe that it is possible to wage war justly. Pacifists believe that a war can never be just.

192. (C) Just War theorists have not offered "citizen consent" as a *necessary* condition to a just war. In other words, Just War theorists are able to imagine a just war occurring even in the absence of complete citizen support.

193. (B) According to the "clean hands" objection, the pacifist's stance involves keeping one's hands clean, morally speaking. In other words, the pacifist adheres to a moral code that keeps one morally blameless, even if doing so comes at the expense of one's own and others' freedom or life.

194. (D) None of the four principles that form the doctrine of double effect explicitly requires consent from those to be affected by the action in question.

195. (A) Torture is generally condemned because, first, most people agree that causing extreme pain in others against their will is generally wrong, and, second, most people agree that breaking down a person's will (destroying his or her autonomy) is wrong.

196. (A) The argument assumes that, if torture is sometimes justified, it then follows that torture ought to be legalized. This assumption ignores the possibility that there are other reasons for not legalizing torture.

197. (E) The phrase *culture of torture* was coined to name an anticipated phenomenon as a consequence of the legalization of torture. This phenomenon would involve an "institutionalization" of torture, a gradual desensitization to the reality of torture, and the creation of a bureaucracy centered entirely around torture.

198. (C) This is the popular "if it's us, it's not terrorism" approach to defining terrorism.

199. (D) Deontological theories of ethics make the related notions of *rights* and *duties* central to their theoretical frameworks.

200. (C) Philosopher and activist Peter Singer wrote this influential article chastising citizens of developed nations for spending money on luxuries rather than on efforts to aid the starving and sick.

201. (B) According to utilitarian theories of ethics, the primary moral obligation humans have is to maximize happiness and minimize misery. Since it is always possible to create even more happiness by making personal sacrifices, utilitarianism seems to demand that one sacrifice everything for the sake of overall happiness. This would, to most people, be too demanding of a moral system.

202. (A) *Beneficence* is typically used to refer to any action intended to bring about well-being in people other than oneself.

203. (E) Consequentialist theories of ethics argue that we ought to perform those acts that have the best consequences. Here, the argument suggests that giving more to charities will have better consequences than not doing so.

204. (E) *Paternalism* is typically used to refer to actions intended to help people without their consent (to being helped).

205. (E) As *paternalism* is typically used to refer to actions intended to help people without their consent, *principle of paternalism* is used to refer to the purported fact that these kinds of actions are sometimes justified.

206. (C) Philosophers typically believe that one is not morally obligated to do what one cannot do, or be reasonably expected to do (*ought* implies *can*). Some critics of Singer's article argue that Singer's moral advice demands more than we can reasonably expect of people, and so the advice cannot be correct.

207. (C) *Supererogation* refers to the practice or act of doing more good than one has a moral duty to do.

208. (B) Singer's article claims that donating more money to charity brings more good into the world than donating less. On the basis of this claim, Singer argues that it then follows that we have a moral obligation to donate more money. Since Singer is basically arguing that we ought to perform a certain action because doing so has better consequences, Singer's argument relies on consequentialism.

209. (C) *Supererogatory* refers to actions that are morally admirable but not obligatory. Giving away all your belongings to a poor family just to help them would typically be regarded as a very nice thing to do, but not something that is morally *required*.

210. (A) Kekes argues that Singer's position involves rampant moralism. By "rampant moralism" Kekes means the intrusion of morally high-minded people who make exaggerated claims about how people ought to behave. Kekes believes Singer's involvement in this intrusion has no rational grounds.

211. (C) Singer argues that both cases involve the same thing: putting one's own luxuries over the life of another human being.

212. (E) Seeing someone suffering might be *psychologically* different from not seeing the sufferer, but it is difficult to understand how proximity or visibility has anything to do with ethical obligations to help those who are suffering.

213. (B) If indeed it were true that, as more privately run charities appear, the extent of government involvement will necessarily lessen, then the claim might have some merit. However, it would be entirely possible for government involvement to remain the same while private organizations chip in as well.

214. (D) Most people agree that doing the right thing can be a very difficult thing to do. Hence, we can expect many people to fail to do the right thing, quite often. But the difficulty of the action simply does not preclude the action from being the morally obligatory one.

215. (E) All forms of euthanasia are deliberate, by definition, so this cannot be a way of classifying a particular manifestation of euthanasia.

216. (B) In general, euthanasia becomes a genuine option for people when they come to believe that it the best and most ethical way to deal with a situation involving extreme physical and psychological pain.

217. (A) *Euthanasia* typically refers to the act or practice of helping someone achieve a wish of ending his or her life to avoid extreme and intolerable suffering.

218. (C) Although it is probably true that euthanasia is bound to cause some upset, this fact is not usually cited as counting against the morality of euthanasia.

219. (D) As of 2011, Oregon is still the only U.S. state in which physician-assisted suicide is legal.

220. (A) According to one of the criteria of the doctrine of double effect, an action with bad consequences cannot be performed, even if it is in order to bring about a good consequence.

221. (D) Practically speaking, the distinction between *active* and *passive* euthanasia is merely semantic. There does not seem to be a big moral difference between unplugging a patient from life support and administering a deadly poison when either act is intended by both patient and doctor to end the patient's life.

222. (A) There exists a widespread fear that an environment in which voluntary euthanasia is legal will make it easier for doctors to give in to the urge to perform involuntary euthanasia without repercussion.

223. (E) There exists little evidence to suggest that suffering, dying patients are necessarily typically incapable of making informed, responsible decisions.

224. (B) There exists little evidence to suggest that doctors inevitably progress from voluntary to involuntary euthanasia whenever voluntary euthanasia becomes legal.

225. (D) Consequentialism is the ethical theory that says that the moral good of an action is determined by its consequences. Hence, if one claims that the moral status of euthanasia depends on what kind of good or bad consequences it has, one adopts a consequentialist view of ethics.

226. (D) Typically, supporters of legalized voluntary euthanasia do not feel that the consent of family members should be required for voluntary euthanasia.

227. (A) Supporters of legalized voluntary euthanasia argue that patients, even when they receive excellent palliative care, are still the ones who must decide whether living with suffering is worth the benefit of being alive. Should they decide it is not, there should be a legal and safe way to act on that decision.

228. (C) Deontological theories of ethics make the related notions of *rights* and *duties* central to their theoretical frameworks.

229. (B) Lasting from 1998 to 2005, the Terri Schiavo case was a legal battle in the United States between the legal guardians and the parents of Teresa Marie "Terri" Schiavo, a patient in a vegetative state.

230. (C) Typically, "pro-lifers" argue that, since a fetus is an innocent person, abortion is akin to murder.

231. (C) Roe v. Wade resulted in a controversial agreement by the United States Supreme Court that a right to privacy under the due process clause in the Fourteenth Amendment extends to a woman's choice to have an abortion.

232. (C) One could even say that pro-lifers are primarily concerned with the rights of the fetus, while pro-choicers are primarily concerned with the rights of the woman.

233. (E) Originality simply isn't original to human beings.

234. (E) Marquis argues that the very thing that makes murder wrong makes abortion wrong.

235. (A) Thomson argued in her influential article that no one has an automatic right to use another person's body as a lifesaving mechanism.

236. (A) Consequentialism is the ethical theory that says that the moral good of an action is determined by its consequences.

237. (A) The article argues that abortion, like murder, robs a being of a "future of value."

238. (A) According to the article, although all persons have a right to life, this right does not entail a right to use someone else's body as a lifesaving mechanism.

239. (B) It could be argued that a complete being with an actual future to speak of does not emerge until conception.

240. (B) The article makes this point with a thought experiment in which someone is imagined to wake up being attached intravenously, without consent, to an ailing violinist who needs constant intravenous connection to that person's body to survive.

241. (A) Thomson claims that while most people would agree that it would be "awfully nice" to refrain from unplugging the violinist, doing so is not a moral obligation.

242. (E) Marquis considers but rejects the notion that murder is wrong because of the bad effects it has on the moral character of the murderer.

243. (E) In the thought experiment, the person who wakes up connected to a violinist could not possibly have foreseen such a turn of events. Sex, however, is widely known to often lead to pregnancy.

244. (B) The fact that men are not expected to change their way of life in response to pregnancy means that there exist different moral expectations from men versus from women (this is what is meant by *double standard*).

245. (E) Tom Beauchamp and James Childress coauthored this important work.

246. (D) Creationism is usually presented as a scientific alternative to the theory of evolution. As such, it is not a theoretical viewpoint available in the field of bioethics.

247. (C) The Hippocratic oath is believed to have been written by Hippocrates, who is sometimes referred to as "the father of Western medicine."

248. (E) As its name implies, bioethics is meant to address ethical issues that arise in the areas of medicine and biology.

249. **(C)** Punctuality, while important in any workplace, is not one of the values in the forefront of medical ethics.

250. **(B)** *Informed consent*, in the context of bioethics, refers to the kind of consent that is freely and rationally given by a patient who has carefully thought about the decision to consent.

251. **(A)** The Declaration of Helsinki was established by the World Medical Association as a statement outlining the ethical principles that are to guide medical research and practice.

252. **(D)** While the case caused much controversy, most people did not think that analyzing the case in terms of *what people deserve* would be of much use.

253. **(A)** The "first do no harm" principle tells us to avoid *maleficence* (doing harm).

254. **(C)** The only point in destroying embryos in the first place is for research. So it would not make sense to destroy embryos if it does not help scientific research.

255. **(B)** *Supererogation* refers to the practice or act of doing more good than one has a strict moral duty to do. Principlism does not require this.

256. **(D)** No current scientific or philosophical theory holds that personal identity and autonomy are entirely determined by genetics.

257. **(B)** The doctrine of double effect lists four conditions that an action with both good and bad effects must have to be morally justified.

258. **(A)** This value is meant to protect the right of patients to make their own decisions about the various aspects of medical treatment.

259. **(E)** Critics typically do not regard affirmative action as presenting a problem of justice to employers. Rather, charges of injustice usually are made in behalf of employees.

260. **(A)** Affirmative action is meant to counter the negative effects of various forms of social discrimination that have occurred in history.

261. **(D)** "Reverse racism" is supposed to refer to the act or practice of giving preferential treatment to groups that have suffered from discrimination in the past.

262. **(E)** According to consequentialist theories of ethics, we have a moral obligation to always act so as to increase the overall balance of well-being over misery.

263. (A) *Preferential selection* is typically used to refer to the act or practice of hiring someone, or accepting someone into a school, not merely on the basis of his or her abilities, but also on the basis of things like race or gender.

264. (A) The phrase *just deserts* is used to refer to whatever it is that a person truly deserves, or actually has a *right* to.

265. (E) Past supporters include Richard Nixon and George H. W. Bush.

266. (D) Typical arguments criticizing affirmative action tend not to address this issue.

267. (E) Many people object to the very idea of hiring someone, or accepting someone into a school, not merely on the basis of his or her abilities, but also on the basis of things like race or gender.

268. (B) JFK's 1961 order mandated "affirmative action to ensure that applicants are employed, and that employees are treated during employment, without regard to their race, creed, color, or national origin."

269. (B). The idea is that out of a pool of equally qualified applicants, one would not expect factors such as race and sex to make a difference in the hiring process. Since they apparently *do* make a difference, quota policies are meant simply to "even things out."

270. (C) *Mismatching*, in the context of issues surrounding affirmative action, refers to the phenomenon of a student's being accepted into a college that requires a higher degree of aptitude than the student possesses.

271. (E) John Rawls is known for, among other things, his theory of justice as *fairness*. Some thinkers have applied Rawls's way of thinking about justice to issues surrounding affirmative action and dealing with the effects of discrimination.

Chapter 4: Political Philosophy

272. (D) In Plato's state, three main social groups exist: those who govern and rule the state, those who protect the state from external and internal threats, and those who produce commodities. Answers (A), (B), (C), and (E) refer to other ways of dividing up a society, but not Plato's.

273. (B) Thrasymachus famously argued in *The Republic* that "justice is the advantage of the stronger." Thrasymachus did not express any of the views given in (A), (C), (D), and (E).

274. (B) Whereas (A), (B), (C), (D), and (E) each present famous Platonic dialogues, (B) is Plato's best-known political work.

275. (E) Plato is often lauded for what seem to be progressive, feminist views. In particular, he is praised for his claim that, in his ideal state, it is one's abilities that determine one's place in society, not one's sex. The points of view expressed in (A), (B), (C), and (D) have each had their own sponsors, but Plato does not number among them.

276. (A) Some have described Plato's state as one that controls every aspect of its subjects' lives, which can seem overly totalitarian. Hence, (B) cannot be the answer. Others have complained that Plato's vision is overly idealized and removed from reality, and so (C) cannot be the answer. Yet others have charged that Plato's attitude toward personal property reeks of communism, which rules out (D) as the answer. Finally, a common complaint about Plato's *Republic* is that it explicitly rules out democratic processes as constituents of its political structure. This rules out (E). So we are left with (A).

277. (C) Plato argued that the ruling class would have to be composed of people who are not concerned with the accumulation of wealth and luxuries, but only with governing wisely and fairly. In order to ensure that only such people gain entry into the ruling class, Plato explicitly states that the ruling class should never be paid as much as the ruled class. Hence, only (C) accurately reflects Plato's position.

278. (C) According to Plato, the soul has a tripartite composition: an appetitive part, a spirited part, and a rational part. This structure is analogous to the structure of Plato's imagined republic, which consists of a producing class (the appetitive part), a protecting class (the spirited part), and a ruling class (the rational part).

279. (A) In *The Republic*, Plato presents his vision of an ideal society, whose members divide into three distinct classes. If you are someone who loves wisdom and wants to pursue wisdom more than anything, then you will belong to the "philosopher king" class, who rule and govern the state. If you are someone who loves and chases after honor, then you will belong to the "guardian" class, who protect the state from internal and external threats. If you want above all to accumulate riches and luxuries, then you will belong to the "producer" class, who produce and exchange commodities.

280. (B) In Plato's vision of the ideal state, it is one's abilities that determine one's place in society, not one's sex. So (A) cannot be the answer. In *The Republic*, Plato has Socrates argue that some amount of deliberate misinformation, propagated by the ruling class, is necessary for the good of the state. So (C) is not the answer. Plato also believed that certain forms of art would not be good for the society and should therefore be banned. This eliminates (D) as an answer. Finally, Plato argued that some of the money collected through taxes ought to be allocated to a public education system, which means that (E) cannot be the answer. This leaves the correct answer, (B). Although the *ruling* classes (the philosopher kings and the guardians) were to have no private property, no such restriction was made by Plato for the ruled class.

281. (E) In *The Republic*, Polemarchus attempts to define *justice* as "giving each his due." Socrates then points out that this definition entails that it would be just to give back a borrowed axe to someone who has recently become mentally ill, knowing that the owner of the axe may hurt himself or others. Since giving back an axe to a deranged person is clearly not the right thing to do, and since justice is necessarily "the right thing to do," Polemarchus's definition cannot be correct, according to Socrates. The examples given in (A) through (D), whether or not they also constitute counterexamples to Polemarchus's definition, are not ones given by Socrates.

282. (B) Much like the ring from *The Lord of the Rings*, Plato's "ring of Gyges" gives its bearer the ability to become invisible, and so to avoid the usual drawbacks to unethical behavior (such as public embarrassment or punishment). Would it make sense to behave ethically even if no one would ever know when we behaved unethically? This is the main question raised by Plato's thought experiment.

283. (B) While Plato imagines that there will be a tendency to follow in the footsteps of one's parents, when it comes to which class one belongs to, Plato also believes that everyone should have the job he or she is best at. So while social roles are generally passed down through the generations, personal capacity is always the final determinant. All answers except for (B) contradict Plato's belief that no one should be stuck with a job he or she is not good at.

284. (E) Early on in *The Republic*, the character Cephalus attempts a definition of *justice* according to which justice is just repaying your debts and speaking the truth. So (A) cannot be the answer. Soon afterward, Polemarchus attempts a definition that defines *justice* as "benefiting your friends and harming your enemies." So (B) is not the answer either. Polemarchus soon changes this definition into "benefiting the just and harming the unjust," which rules out (C). Finally, Thrasymachus famously gives his "might makes right" definition of justice, according to which *justice* means "the advantage of the strongest." Since this rules out (D), we are left with (E), which gives a definition not given anywhere in *The Republic*.

285. (B) Aristotle conceives his subject matter in the *Nicomachean Ethics* as being the most authoritative subject, political science. It deals with the ordering of the state and households, and regulative principles of human behavior. It breaks down further into the headings of ethics and political philosophy.

286. (C) Aristotle conceives of politics as basically involved with crafting laws, learning to work within a system to make the best expression of principles. This is expressed by analogy with a craftsman.

287. (A) Although constitutions are expressed as written documents, Aristotle sees constitutions as most basically an abstract organizing principle that determines the form that a community takes. This is a very important role, and not a mere formality. (D) need not necessarily describe how a constitution comes about. (E) would be akin to a platonic form, which Aristotle does not countenance.

288. (D) Aristotle thought that the system of slavery was beneficial to slaves, who, lacking the capacity to make good decisions for themselves (so he thought), need someone to order their lives for them. It was thus not based on any natural right of the master, but rather was for the benefit of the enslaved, similarly to how a social and political order itself is arranged for the benefit of the ruled citizenry.

289. (D) An oligarchy is ruled by a small ruling class that concentrates too much power unto itself. Aristotle thought that this type of government tended to take the shape of the wealthiest using their economic power in the form of political power. This group of individuals would not necessarily have noble blood, be the cultural elite, or exercise religious authority.

290. (B) Aristotle thought that since the goal of the state is to maximize the good life in virtue among its inhabitants, whatever system accomplishes this in the best way is what is to be preferred. He thought that an aristocracy, literally rule by the "best men," is the best way to promote virtue generally. Most men, he thought, are relatively non-virtuous, so rule by democracy would not tend to promote virtue generally. An oligarchy is a bad version of an aristocracy, in which rule is based on the power of wealth. In most monarchies, power is too concentrated in the hands of one man, and for this reason a government consisting of as many virtuous men as possible would be optimal.

291. (E) Aristotle thought that a city-state should ideally be directed toward promotion of virtue, which according to Aristotle constitutes the good life. He further thought that the good life is best promoted by an aristocracy, in which the most virtuous individuals rule. This is in contrast with what oligarchs would have, which is to maximize the creation of wealth, and a warrior ruling class, which would build up a city to be as militarily strong as possible. It is also in contrast to a pure democracy, in which pure liberty is valued for its own sake.

292. (A) Aristotle thought that even in cases where most people taken individually are not as virtuous as moral aristocrats, they may be more virtuous if put together and taken as an operating whole. In this case, the virtue of people taken collectively might be superior to those of an aristocracy. It is only for this reason that Aristotle is willing to countenance any political system: to him, the highest good furthered by the state is the promotion of virtue generally, so in principle he would be in favor of any system that he thought would best achieve that end.

293. (A) Plato wrote during the first half of the 4th century BCE, at a time of great intellectual foment in Athens. He was a student of Socrates, who lived at the end of the 5th century BCE, and wrote many influential dialogues in which his teacher Socrates figured as the principal character.

294. (B) Aristotle was a student of Plato and wrote in the second half of the 4th century BCE. Although he came to disagree with much that his teacher taught, Aristotle carried on many similar themes to those on which Plato wrote.

295. (D) According to Hobbes, if we did not have social rules, we would behave more or less like animals, and life would be, in his words, "solitary, poor, nasty, brutish, and short." Hobbes calls this primal, dog-eat-dog situation a state of nature. The other answers involve different concepts related to Hobbes's political philosophy.

296. (A) The correct answer defines *social contract theory* as a political theory that holds that the only legitimate basis for political authority is one of mutual consent. (B) is incorrect because social contract theory does not necessesarily require that all members of the society *explicitly* consent to the laws in order for them to be legitimate. (C) is incorrect because it describes Plato's noncontractarian model of government. (D) and (E) are incorrect, not because they necessarily conflict with social contract theory, but because they simply do not accurately describe the theory.

297. (E) According to Hobbes, three basic forms of government are possible: aristocracy, democracy, and monarchy. Hobbes believed that aristocracy and democracy are both so flawed that they inevitably invite civil war, which invariably leads to the dissolution of the political system. Hobbes did not think monarchy was similarly flawed. None of the claims given in (A) through (D) accurately portray Hobbes's argument for the superiority of monarchy.

298. (A) The process wherein individuals unite into political societies through mutual consent involves entering into what Hobbes and other theorists have called a social contract. (B) is incorrect because this phrase describes the conditions in which we find ourselves *before* entering into a social contract. (C) is incorrect because the notion of consent is only one *part* of a social contract, and it need not be tacit. (D) is incorrect because it involves the notion of *war*, which would not make sense in describing the process of entering, through mutual consent, into political societies. Likewise, (E) is incorrect because it involves a notion (anarchy) unlikely to constitute a proper part of the process of forming political societies.

299. (D) Hobbes's most famous work, in which he presents his social contract theory, is called *Leviathan* (after the monster described in the Bible). About a century after Hobbes's work, Rousseau wrote *The Social Contract*. *The Republic* is Plato's famous political treatise. *A Theory of Justice*, by John Rawls, is arguably the most influential political work of the 20th century. *Nichomachean Ethics* is Aristotle's treatise on ethics.

300. (D) While Hobbes's "twelve rights of the sovereign" do not explicitly state that sovereigns may be prevented from changing the original contract, neither do they explicitly give sovereigns the right not to be prevented from doing so. Each of the other answers corresponds to one of the 12 rights outlined in *Leviathan*.

301. (C) According to Locke, there are three basic forms of government: the rule of one (monarchy), the rule of the few (aristocracy), and the rule of the many (democracy). A monarchy that is disapproved of is called by its subjects a tyranny. An aristocracy that is disapproved of is called an oligarchy. A democracy that is disapproved of is called anarchy. Of the possible answers, only (C) correctly makes the proper distinctions held by Locke.

302. (C) Locke believed that there were certain rules that apply equally to all individuals, no matter who they are or where they live (it is useful here to think of our contemporary notion of basic "human rights"). Locke called the set of these rules *natural law*. Locke also believed that there were other types of rules that are created through mutual consent. These rules, which may be different depending on the people that created them, are called *conventional law* (or sometimes *positive law*). (A), (B), (D), and (E) make different distinctions between types of law, but none captures Locke's particular distinction.

303. (D). (A), (B), (C), and (E) each describe what Locke thought of as basic duties, to which all our behavior must comply. Locke does not argue, however, that causing unhappiness to others is always in conflict with our basic duties. Hence, (D) is the correct answer.

304. (E) Locke's *Two Treatises* relies neither on utilitarianism (the ethical theory according to which we ought to maximize happiness and minimize suffering) nor on divine command theory (the ethical theory according to which God is the creator of moral laws), so (A) cannot be the right answer. Neither does it rely on Machiavelli's famous work, so (B) is out as well. The notions of anarchy (the absence of rule) and libertarianism (the political theory according to which individual liberty constitutes the most basic moral principle) do not form the basis of *Two Treatises* either; hence, (C) is incorrect. Finally, Locke did not base his great work on Plato's *Republic*, so (D) is wrong as well. Only (E) correctly identifies the two basic pillars of Locke's *Two Treatises*: social contract theory (the theory according to which legitimate governments arise out of a social contract between mutually consenting individuals) and natural rights theory (the theory according to which all individuals have basic, unalienable rights—think of the American Constitution, which was heavily influenced by Locke's ideas).

305. (C) Locke believed a government can only be legitimate when it is the product of a social contract between mutually consenting individuals. This rules out the possibility of justifying a government by way of things like "divine rights." Hence, (A), (B), (D), and (E) do not accurately describe Locke's beliefs about the relation between the "divine right of kings" and the justification of government.

306. (A) Concerning property rights, Locke argues that we have a basic right to ownership of our own bodies (which is why it is wrong to just lock someone up for no reason). This right extends to any work we do with our bodies (which is why slavery is wrong), according to Locke. Locke then maintains that whatever is the product of the work we do with our own bodies is our rightful property. So private property is a right whenever that property involves products we brought about through our own labor. None of the premises given in (B) through (D) is involved in this argument, but the one given in (A) is.

307. (D) Locke believed in the right of citizens to revolt if they feel that the government is corrupt in some way. He also believed that we have a right to private property when it comes to things created by our own labor. Locke was also a social contract theorist (like Hobbes, who first introduced the notion of a "state of nature"). Finally, Locke believed that all individuals share the same set of basic human rights. This leaves us with (D), which is incorrect because Locke explicitly denounces the notion of the divine right of kings.

308. (C) The 17th-century British philosopher Thomas Hobbes (1588–1679) was one of the founders of modern political philosophy. His central work, *Leviathan*, put forth his views of the significance of political power over against what would otherwise be man's "state of nature," which he famously said would in an anarchic state be "solitary, poor, nasty, brutish, and short."

309. (D) The 17th-century British philosopher John Locke's (1632–1704) work of political philosophy, *Two Treatises of Government*, partly carried on a tradition of social contract theory among British political philosophers that Thomas Hobbes was also a part of.

310. (C) Mill did not base his theories on deontology (a duty-based view of ethics). Neither did Mill build on virtue ethics (the view of ethics according to which *moral character* is of primary importance in ethics). Mill also did not base his views on divine command theory (the theory of ethics according to which God is the creator of moral laws). Finally, Mill did not theorize on the basis of relativism (the theory that holds that whether an action is morally good or bad is relative to some standard of evaluation). Instead, Mill was working within a largely *consequentialist* context. According to consequentialism, whether an action is right or wrong depends on the consequences of that action.

311. (B) According to Mill, the right to liberty is a basic human right that may not be violated, *unless* that liberty is restricted in order to prevent an individual from harming others. Hence, the other answers do not accurately describe Mill's views on the restriction of personal liberty.

312. (E) Out of the possible answers, (E) stands out, since it is difficult to see how this claim could possibly function as a premise in an argument against censorship. Each of the other premises makes more sense and accurately describes Mill's views on the subject.

313. (D) In his work *On Liberty*, Mill argues that every individual is "sovereign" over his own mind and body. For this reason, Mill opposes situations in which the majority of a society imposes its moral beliefs upon others, when doing so conflicts with this sovereignty. Mill dubbed such a scenario "the tyranny of the majority." The other answers involve various vaguely related notions, but only (D) correctly identifies the phrase used by Mill.

314. (E) According to Mill, individuals should not have their freedoms constrained in any way, unless it is done to prevent harm to others. Hence, for Mill, liberty should be understood as the right to do whatever one wants, as long as doing so does not harm others. (A) is therefore wrong, since it involves unrestricted freedom. (B) presents a possible definition of liberty, but it does not represent Mill's philosophical views on liberty. (C) also involves a possible definition, but, again, it does not represent Mill's ideas about liberty. Finally, (D) is a view on the empirical possibility of liberty, but Mill's work does not contain this conjecture. Only (E) accurately reflects Mill's position on personal liberty.

315. (B) *Paternalism* means, in this context, "limiting someone's freedom for his or her own good." So the answer cannot be (C), (D), or (E). Mill explicitly denounces the practice of limiting individual liberty for the individual's own good, so (A) is incorrect. Hence, (B) is the answer.

316. (D) Jean-Jacques Rousseau is the author of *The Social Contract*, written about a century after Thomas Hobbes wrote *Leviathan*. *The Republic* is Plato's famous political treatise, and *Republicanism* was written in the late 20th century by Philip Pettit. *A Theory of Justice*, arguably the most influential political work of the 20th century, was written by John Rawls.

317. (D) In Rawls's version of social contract theory, just laws are those that would be agreed upon by suitably situated, free, rational, and equal people. For Rawls, "suitably situated" means that the individuals are to have no knowledge about their own and others' social statuses vis-à-vis things such as sex, race, religion, and so on, in deciding which laws to agree to. Hence, out of the all the answers, only (D) accurately describes Rawls's "veil of ignorance."

318. (C) Rawls presents a theory of justice in which justice is primarily understood as a form of fairness. Although "liberty" is no doubt an important concept for Rawls, it is not how he understands justice. Likewise, basic rights are important to Rawls's overall project, but the notion of "justice as a basic right" is not how Rawls presents his theory of justice. The Kantian notion of a categorical imperative may indeed relate in some interesting way to the notion of justice, but, again, it is not an essentially Rawlsian notion. Finally, utility, or aptness at achieving some desired end, is a utilitarian notion not at all of central importance to Rawls's account of justice.

319. (A) (B) involves an appeal to utilitarian principles, not of central interest to Rawls's project. So (B) is incorrect. (C) involves an appeal to a Kantian principle, also not of central importance to Rawls. (D) describes a version of libertarianism, which would not be an accurate portrayal of Rawls's theory. Finally, (E), while similar in form to the correct answer, presents a distorted account of Rawls's theory.

320. (D) Four of the objections presented in (A) through (E) have been raised at various times by various respected authors, but the objection that the Rawlsian theory of justice fails to treat aspects of game theory that deal with human psychology has not made its appearance in the relevant literature (in fact, it's made-up!).

321. (E) Where Hobbes has us imagine a "state of nature" in order to see the rationale of agreeing to a social contract, Rawls encourages us to contemplate an "original position." The original position involves not knowing what sex, race, religion, and so on, one will be in the new society (hence, the original position is behind a "veil of ignorance"). This way, there is more of a guarantee that the laws will be fair. (A), therefore, is incorrect because this is Hobbes's notion. (B) is incorrect because this is the myth discussed in Plato's *Republic*. (C) is wrong because the social contract is what individuals agree to from *within* the hypothetical situation behind the veil of ignorance, not the situation itself. Finally, (D) is incorrect because the hedonistic calculus is a notion proper to utilitarianism and is not directly or essentially related to Rawls's theory.

322. (E) Rawls's second (of two) "Principle of Justice" states, in part, that social and economic inequalities are to be of the greatest benefit to the least advantaged members of society. This part of the principle is usually referred to as "the difference principle." Out of the possible answers, only (E) accurately describes the difference principle.

323. (C) Freedom is an important concept for Rawls, but personal liberty does not entail a right to get rid of one's own basic rights. In other words, Rawls does not think, for example, that the freedom to sell oneself into slavery constitutes a primary good. Whereas the freedoms and rights referred to in (A), (B), (D), and (E) are regarded by Rawls as primary goods, (C), then, is not.

324. (B) The 19th-century British philosopher J. S. Mill (1806–1873), in his greatly influential work *On Liberty*, championed the rights of the individual in society to do whatever does not harm others.

325. (E) The 20th-century American philosopher John Rawls (1921–2002) initiated a novel and influential theory of justice that was first introduced in his 1957 article "Justice as Fairness" and culminated in the 1971 publication of *A Theory of Justice*.

Chapter 5: Philosophy of Religion

326. (D) Most traditional theists do not attribute to God the ability to transcend logic. So, for example, the fact that God cannot create an object so heavy that He cannot lift it is not generally thought to contradict God's omnipotence, since the impossibility here is a logical impossibility. By contrast, theists do tend to believe that God is not bound by the laws of physics, so (B) is not the correct answer. Omnipotence (being all-powerful), omniscience (being all-knowing), and omnibenevolence (being all-good) are also traditionally associated with the God of theism, ruling out (A), (C), and (E).

327. (A) The theist's God is usually thought of as both *immanent* and *transcendent*. God's immanence entails that He acts directly, and in historical time, on His creation. God's transcendence entails that God's existence is not limited to the confines of His own creation, but rather that He exists also beyond the realm of physical existence. By contrast, the deist's God is wholly transcendent. This means that the God of deism may have initially created the physical universe and its inhabitants but does not interfere with His creation after the original creative act.

328. (E) The view typically associated with *dualism* is that reality can be divided into two basic types of substance (typically *mind* and *matter*, but other conceptions exist as well), which does not say that God is one with the universe, so (A) is incorrect. *Deism* is a conception of God according to which God exists wholly beyond the physical realm of His creation, which directly contradicts the notion of God's unity with the universe, so (B) cannot be correct. The *mind-body identity* thesis mentioned in (C) refers to the belief that the mind and the brain are the same thing, which does not necessarily entail the belief that God and the universe are the same thing. *Naturalism* is a way of thinking about reality according to which nothing supernatural exists, or is assumed to exist, which also does not necessarily commit one to a belief in the identity of God and the universe. This rules out (D), leaving us with (E), *pantheism*.

329. (C) In contrast with *positive theology*, according to which we can attribute positive, knowable qualities to God, *negative theology* (or *via negativa*) holds that we can refer to God only by means of qualities that He does *not* possess.

330. (A) According to *reformed epistemology*, certain beliefs are (in Plantinga's terms) *properly basic*. These are beliefs that one is rational in having, even if there is no positive evidence for the belief. For example, the belief that other human beings have conscious minds like yours has no positive proof for its truth, and yet it is rational to have that belief. Likewise, reformed epistemologists argue, the belief in God is rational, even though it is derived from other known truths.

331. (E) An atheist is simply a person who lacks a belief in any god. Such a person may or may not have additional beliefs about the knowability of the existence or nonexistence of God, so (A) is not the right answer. A skeptic is someone who demands strong evidence for a belief, or simply someone who is doubtful about some particular belief or set of beliefs. Such a person may believe that God's existence or nonexistence is knowable and yet still be properly called a skeptic, which means that (B) is also incorrect. *Naturalist* can mean several things, but in the context of a discussion about religious belief, it usually refers to a person who believes that only the natural world exists. Being a naturalist does not prevent one from believing that God's existence or nonexistence is knowable. Hence, (C) is not right either. A scientist is simply someone who practices science, and whether one is a scientist need have no bearing on one's beliefs about the knowability of God's existence or nonexistence, so (D) is ruled out as well. This means that the correct answer is (E), *agnostic*. Strictly speaking, an agnostic can be either a theist or an atheist, since agnosticism is a position concerning *knowledge* about God, while theism and atheism concern *belief* about God.

332. (C) According to *fideism*, although many or most truths are arrived at via reason and testable empirical evidence, some truths can be apprehended only through faith.

333. (D) *Theism* is the belief in the existence of God. *Atheism* is the lack of such a belief. *Agnosticism* is the belief that the truth concerning God's existence or nonexistence cannot be known. You could *believe* that God exists, without thinking that you *know* that God exists. Or you could *not believe* that God exists, without thinking that you *know* that God does not exist. Hence, one could be an atheist or a theist and still be an agnostic.

334. (D) W. K. Clifford argues in his *Ethics of Belief* that it is always wrong to believe something on the basis of insufficient evidence. William James critiques this view in his *The Will to Believe*. Both of these works have been hugely influential in subsequent discussions concerning the ethics of belief.

335. (D) A *live* option (for a belief) is one that appears a genuine possibility to the person contemplating the belief. The requirement that the belief be *live* is therefore the requirement that it be relatively *believable* to the potential believer. The requirement that the belief be *forced* means that the potential believer must make a choice as to whether to believe. If there are more options than believing or not believing, the choice to believe is not genuinely forced. The *momentous* requirement holds that the situation in which one is required to make a choice in one's beliefs is unique and that the choice is significant in one's life. If each of these conditions is met, according to James, then it is not morally wrong to have a belief for which one does not have sufficient evidence.

336. (A) In his essay *Ethics of Belief*, Clifford defends the view that holding a belief for reasons other than that the belief is supported by sufficient evidence is in all circumstances immoral.

337. (D) Epistemology is a subfield in philosophy having to do with the nature and possibility of knowledge. Ethics is concerned with questions about morality and goodness. Logic studies the formal properties of arguments. Metaphysics deals with fundamental questions concerning existence and reality. Aesthetics is concerned with art and the nature of beauty. Given these characterizations of the major branches of philosophy, out of these options, metaphysics is most directly relevant to the question of the existence of God.

338. (A) In his works on metaphysics, Aristotle postulates the existence of a primary cause for all motion in the universe. This primary cause causes other things to move, without it itself moving. According to Aristotle, this entity simply contemplates its own contemplation, and in so doing, it inspires the universe into motion. Many philosophers have found it natural to interpret this *unmoved mover* as God, or at least a possible conception of God.

339. (C) *Absolutism* typically refers to the theory that there exists a single moral code that applies to all beings equally, regardless of historical epoch or culture. One can be an absolutist without believing that God is the author of this code, so (A) is incorrect. Theism is the belief that God exists, but this need not involve the further belief that God is literally the creator of morality. Hence, the answer cannot be (B). According to social contract theory, whether something is wrong or right is determined by whether the action obeys the rules we have all agreed to live by, so (D) must be wrong. Virtue ethics is an approach to ethics according to which whether an action is good depends on whether a person with a perfectly moral character would do that action in those circumstances. So (E) is also erroneous. Hence, (C) is correct.

340. (C) According to traditional theism, God transcends the natural world and often reveals Himself in it as well. This is the view that God transcends the world and is partially immanent. According to deism, God transcends the natural world and never intervenes in it. This is the view that God transcends the world and is not immanent at all. According to pantheism, God is identical with the natural world, and so God is wholly immanent and not at all transcendent. Finally, according to panentheism, God is both wholly immanent and transcendent. Options (D) and (E) do not correspond to any traditional forms of belief in God. So (C) gives the correct answer.

341. (A) Natural theology can be distinguished from *transcendental theology*, which proceeds from *a priori* reasoning, and from *revealed theology*, which proceeds from supernatural revelation. Unlike transcendental and revealed theology, natural theology is based on everyday experience and reason. Answers (B) through (E) do not correspond to *any* of these main traditional forms of theology.

342. (B) The famous poem attributed to the blind Greek poet is *The Odyssey*, not *Theodicy*, so (A) is incorrect. The belief that human beings can refer to God only by way of what God is *not* describes *negative theology*, which means (C) is not the answer. There is no special branch of study devoted solely to the task of reconciling religion with science, so (D) can be ruled out. Finally, theology that proceeds from *a priori* reasoning is known as *transcendental theology*, so (E) is also incorrect.

343. (E) Natural theology is a branch of theology that relies on reason and ordinary experience. *Theodicy* refers to attempts to answer the problem of evil (the apparent incompatibility between the existence of evil and God's goodness). Revealed theology is a branch of theology based on scripture and religious experience (i.e., theology through revelation). Pantheism is the view that God is identical with the natural world. Only the last option correctly names the branch of theology based on *a priori* reasoning.

344. (E) *A posteriori* arguments for the existence of God are based on empirical evidence, rather than on reason alone (as are *a priori* arguments). Out of the options given, only the *ontological argument* is a purely *a priori*, reason-based, argument.

345. (B) The answer is hidden in the name: *cosmological* refers to the cosmos, or the universe. Each of the other answers gives a different well-known argument for the existence of God, but only (B) correctly names the argument that attempts to derive God's existence from the very existence of the universe.

346. (C) Anselm's *ontological* proof for the existence of God, given in his *Proslogion*, is typically held to be the first complete formulation of the ontological argument.

347. (B) According to Pascal, even if the evidence for or against God's existence is not conclusive, a rational person would choose to believe in God anyway. The reason for this is as follows: If you believe in God, then you are either correct or incorrect. If you are incorrect, you do not suffer any great loss. If you are correct, you gain an infinite good (eternity in heaven). Moreover, if you do not believe in God, then you are either correct or incorrect. If you are incorrect, you suffer an infinite loss (eternity in hell). If you are correct, you do not gain any great good. Either way, you are better off believing.

348. (E) Teleological arguments for the existence of God typically rely on two types of premises: (1) The existence of complex purposeful artifacts like watches, computers, cars, and so on, can only be explained with reference to intelligent, conscious designers. (2) The existence of a high degree of complexity and purpose of natural objects can likewise only be explained with reference to an intelligent, conscious designer (i.e., God). Each of the options falls into one or the other of these two categories, with the exception of (E), which does not involve reference to anything highly complex or purposeful.

349. (D) In fact, David Hume was critical of the ontological argument and presented an objection prefiguring Kant's famous criticism.

350. (B) Moral arguments for the existence of God typically point to the apparent objectivity of moral standards as something that can only be explained supernaturally (i.e., through a deity, like God). The other options listed are made-up arguments.

351. (A) Arguments from reason typically point out that, on a purely natural scheme, there is no reason to suppose that human beings ever know the truth about the world around them, since our beliefs would have been caused by blind, physical processes that do not care about "truth." Hence, the argument goes, if naturalism were true, we would never know it.

352. (A) According to the Kalām version of the cosmological argument, everything that begins to exist must have a cause, and since the universe began to exist, it must have a cause, and this cause is identical with God.

353. (E) Teleological arguments for the existence of God often proceed by way of analogy to human agents and their created artifacts. In this version of the argument, the analogy is from human civil laws, which require intelligent lawmakers (human persons), to natural laws, which then seem to require an intelligent lawmaker (God) as well.

354. (C) According to the anthropic argument for the existence of God, the universe seems to be "fine-tuned" to support life, and the best explanation for this fine-tuning is the existence of a supernatural being (God).

355. (C) Although there is an argument for the existence of God known as the "moral argument," that argument was not included in Aquinas's set of "five ways."

356. (C) William Paley, in his 1802 work, *Natural Theology*, points out that upon coming across an artifact like a watch, which appears to be designed for a particular purpose, we naturally assume it must have had a designer. Likewise, Paley's argument continues, if we come across a natural artifact that appears to be designed for a particular purpose, it makes good sense to suppose that some intelligent being must have designed it for that purpose.

357. (E) The argument that God must have fine-tuned the laws of the universe in order to bring about the possibility of life, and human life in particular, is known as the *anthropic argument* for the existence of God (or sometimes just the *fine-tuning argument*).

358. (D) Euthyphro's dilemma concerns the two possible answers to the question "Does God have reasons for approving of good actions, or not?" If God has reasons, then it is those reasons that make the action good, and not God's approval. If God does not have reasons for His approval, then God is capricious and arbitrary, which is contrary to the traditional definition of God. Neither of these options is palatable to those who believe morality is literally created by God.

359. (B) According to the ontological argument, since the perfect conceivable being could not lack the property of existence, or it would not be perfect, the perfect conceivable being must exist. Kant famously rejects the premise of this argument on the grounds that "exists" is not a real predicate like, for example, "is red" or "is heavy."

360. (D) Cosmological arguments are often of the following form: (1) Everything that begins to exist must have a cause outside of itself. (2) The universe began to exist. Therefore, (3) the universe must have a cause outside of itself. This argument is then presented as a proof for the existence of God, typically understood as a personal deity. The missing premise here is "The cause of the universe is a supernatural person," which may not be an acceptable premise, as the criticism presented in (D) alleges.

361. (C) The quote is often attributed directly to Nietzsche himself. In fact, however, Nietzsche has different characters (in different books) make the claim, which concerns not the literal death of God but the death of the cultural paradigm of belief in God.

362. (D) Prior to Darwin's theory of evolution by natural selection, it was very difficult to explain the apparent design and purposiveness of earth's life-forms. This difficulty lent some support to the notion that a very intelligent, supernatural entity must have designed biological organisms to be just how they are, since we typically explain design and purpose in terms of intelligent agents. For those who accept the theory of evolution, the supernatural hypothesis is typically seen as gratuitous and unnecessary.

363. (C) The God of traditional theism is typically believed to possess omniscience, omnipotence, and omnibenevolence. According to the problem of evil, these attributes seem incompatible with the existence of suffering, especially pointless suffering caused by natural, nonhuman forces.

364. (B) Teleological arguments for the existence of God typically infer the presence of an intelligent designer from the presence of complexity or functionality. Critics have pointed out that other explanations may be available (such as the theory of evolution, in the case of biological complexity) and that therefore not all cases of complexity or purposiveness need to be explained in terms of intentional design.

365. (D) Cosmological arguments typically argue from the existence of the universe to the necessity of a transcendent cause of the universe. (A), (B), (C), and (E) present objections to these types of argument. (D), however, simply states a purported fact about the universe and does not present any special difficulties for cosmological arguments (in fact, the finite universe posited by the big bang theory is often welcomed by theists as a point in favor of an act of special creation by a supernatural creator).

366. (B) According to this argument, if human beings truly have free will, then there are possible universes in which we freely choose to do good, all the time. Since God is omnipotent, He could have picked any possible world to become the actual world, and so He could have selected the world in which people always choose to do good, of their own free will.

367. (E) This argument points out there exists, and has existed throughout time, a significant portion of the population, consisting of rational and open-minded seekers of truth, that does not see any persuasive reason to believe in God. If God exists, the argument continues, it is difficult to see how He would allow this kind of reasonable unbelief to occur, especially to the possible detriment of the reasonable unbeliever.

368. (C) Atheists are sometimes called upon to prove that God does not exist. Bertrand Russell's reply to such demands can be paraphrased as follows: Suppose I believe that a flying teapot revolves around Mars. It would then be unreasonable for me to expect doubters to *prove* that there is no flying teapot orbiting Mars. Rather, the burden of proof would be on me to show that there really is such a teapot. Likewise, atheists cannot reasonably be expected to justify their nonbelief. Rather, the burden of proof is on the theist's side to show that there really is a perfect supernatural person.

369. (C) *Moral evil* refers to any evil or suffering brought about by intentional actions on the part of morally responsible agents. According to the free will defense, God does not typically prevent moral evil, since doing so would interfere with our free will. Under this argument, a world in which we do not have free will is necessarily worse than one in which we do have free will, so God has given us free will. In this way, the free will defense seeks to show that God's goodness is compatible with the existence of moral evil after all.

370. (D). (A), (B), (C), and (E) each presents a claim that is directly relevant to the claim that religion is responsible for much evil. (D), however, merely cites the "problem of evil," which is not a relevant counterargument here (especially since that problem is typically seen as a criticism of theistic belief).

371. (C) *Omniscience* denotes the attribute of being all-knowing. It is often argued that if God knows everything, then He already knows, before we even act, exactly which actions we will take. This seems to contradict *free will*, the notion that whatever we do, we could have done otherwise. So, many people conclude that if God is omniscient, free will does not exist.

372. (A) According to Gould, the *magisterium* of science is concerned with the natural world and addresses questions concerning empirical matters, while the *magisterium* of religion is concerned with questions of ultimate meaning and morality. Since the two magisteria have different subject matters altogether (they do not "overlap"), there is no possibility of contradiction between the two.

373. (B) The view described in (A) is a substantive theory about what actually exists, known as *metaphysical naturalism*. Hence, (A) is incorrect. Option (C) does not describe any serious view in the philosophy of religion (it is just a made-up view), so that is not the correct answer. (D) just describes the God of deism, and (E) simply summarizes various forms of creationism, so neither of those answers is correct. The correct answer, then, is (B).

374. (D) Before Darwin, it was assumed that species do not change, but rather, as stated in the Bible, each creature reproduces "after its own kind." These "kinds," it was assumed, were created by God when He first brought life into being. Darwin's theory of evolution by natural selection showed that the differences between species are not fixed and can be explained naturalistically.

375. (E) Option (E) cannot be the correct answer, since Hume famously argued that the link between cause and effect is not a necessary one. If the existence of miracles really did imply the truth of this thesis, Hume obviously would not have held that to be an objection to belief in miracles.

376. (C) Although he is also a famous atheist, Mackie is not one of the "four horsemen."

377. (D) Memes are sometimes characterized as being the cultural equivalents to *genes*, since memes, like genes, can reproduce themselves, mutate, and evolve to respond to selective pressures. Memes reproduce themselves by spreading from one mind to another, rather like a virus.

378. (E) Logical positivism, a philosophical movement that flourished during the first half of the 20th century, typically adhered to one or both of the following criteria of meaningfulness: (1) verifiability—a claim must be in principle subject to verification to be considered meaningful, and (2) falsifiability—a claim must be in principle subject to falsification to be considered meaningful. According to many supporters of logical positivism, religious claims fail both of these criteria, and so they cannot be considered genuinely meaningful.

379. (B) The scientific method proceeds by gathering data about the natural world and then forming naturalistic explanations for the data. Hence, the method does not require that one give up supernatural beliefs, only that these beliefs do not interfere with the scientific work being done. This means that the naturalism inherent in science is merely *methodological*. The more substantive view, *metaphysical naturalism*, which says that nothing supernatural exists, pairs nicely with the scientific approach to gathering knowledge but is not logically entailed by it.

Chapter 6: Metaphysics

380. (A) According to the theory of supervenience, there is a dependency relation between the mental and the physical. On this theory, the mental *supervenes* on the physical, so that any change in mental states necessarily involves a change in those physical states that give rise to mental events.

381. (C) Substance dualism is the view that reality divides into two basic types of things. Usually, this view is expressed as the claim that anything that exists must be either a mental substance or a physical substance.

382. (E) Although *materialism* is often used interchangeably with *physicalism*, strictly speaking, *materialism* is the view that nothing exists but matter, whereas *physicalism* is the view that nothing exists but the physical world, as it is described by physics (which means that things quite different from traditional "matter" may exist, such as *quarks*, *strings*, and *membranes*).

383. (C) According to Berkeley, *"esse est percipi,"* which means "to be is to be perceived." Berkeley essentially argued that the external, physical world depends for its existence on our (or God's) experience of it.

384. (B) Like substance dualism, property dualism claims that the mental does exist. Unlike substance dualism, however, property dualism holds that the mental can exist only as a *property* of physical things.

385. (D) According to the identity theory of mind, mental states are identical to physical states. This means that mental states and physical states are one and the same, which entails that the mental and the physical cannot constitute fundamentally different substances.

386. (C) According to Chalmers, questions like (A), (B), (D), and (E) are "easy," because these are questions that can be answered by specifying some physical mechanism that can fulfill the function asked about, whereas (C) is a question that remains even after all the physical mechanisms have been specified.

387. (D) It is typically agreed that we have the capacity for complex mental tasks, such as cogitating, distinguishing between different sounds, identifying things in our visual field, and responding intelligently to various stimuli. Some philosophers, however, believe that each of these tasks, when carried out, also brings with it certain subjective "feels" that are available only to the agent performing the task. These raw "feels" are often referred to as *qualia*.

388. (A) Etymologically, *monism* is related to the word *mono*, and both are derived from the Greek word *monos*, meaning "single." Both *idealism* and classic *materialism* are examples of monistic metaphysics.

389. (D) Because zombies are physically exactly like us, but they lack consciousness while we do not, they must not be *entirely* identical to us. This seems to imply that there is more to us than our physical makeup, which is contrary to what physicalism supposes.

390. (B) *Epiphenomenalism*, in the context of dualism, is the view that mental substances have no causal power over physical substances. *Parallelism*, in this context, is the view that God guarantees a coordination between mental occurrences and physical occurrences, even though both occur separately, in different substances. According to *occasionalism*, mental substances and physical substances do not interact, but God causes all events in both substances. *Interactionism* says that mental substances and physical substances can interact with one another. *Functionalism* is the view that mental states are constituted by the functional role in a physical system, and so it denies that the mental constitutes a separate substance from the physical.

391. (D) In the thought experiment, Mary is a scientist who knows all the physical facts there are to know about color, but because she has lived her entire life in a black and white room, she has never *experienced* color. The popular intuition that Mary would have learned something new upon experiencing color for the first time seems to suggest that there is more to knowing about color than knowing all the physical facts about it. Since *physicalism* is often described as the view that the only facts there are, are physical facts, the thought experiment is typically considered a counterexample to physicalism.

392. (B) Functionalism is a physicalist theory of mind, often put forth as an alternative to other contemporary theories of mind, such as behaviorism and identity theory. According to functionalism, mental states can best be explained and described in terms of the functional roles they play in a larger physical system.

393. (E) Answer (E) could not possibly constitute a problem for substance dualism, since substance dualism does not claim or imply that subjective properties emerge out of objective properties.

394. (E) Epiphenomenalism is a stance concerning the causal relation between the mental and the physical, where the mental is held to be causally inert. In contemporary discussion of the philosophy of mind, epiphenomenalism tends to be something of which one is *accused*, rather than something one defends willingly.

395. (B) Paul and Patricia Churchland are probably the most well-known representatives of eliminative materialism. Although the difference between eliminative materialism and identity theory is not always clear, eliminative materialists tend to be more comfortable entirely denying the reality or coherence of many of our "commonsense" psychological notions, whereas identity theorists may simply claim that such notions concern real states but that these states are entirely physical.

396. (D) According to Hume, causality is not something that exists independently in the world. Rather, whenever we notice that one type of event always follows another event, we say that one is the cause of the other.

397. (C) If one thinks of *determining* as *causing*, the term *overdetermination* is rather self-explanatory. To be precise, however, one should think of an overdetermined event as an event that has more than one *sufficient* cause.

398. (D) An object's *final cause* is its proper purpose or function. An object's *efficient cause* is whatever caused it come into being in the first place. An object's *material cause* is whatever it is made of. An object's *formal cause* is its form or functional structure.

399. (D) If human actions truly did not have causes that are sufficient to bring them about, then there would exist some events (i.e., human actions) that are not determined. If such events existed, the universe would not be wholly deterministic.

400. (B) Laplace's demon is often used as a kind of symbol for the classic mechanistic model of a completely deterministic universe.

401. (D) A *sufficient* cause is a cause that is *enough* to bring about its effects, though not necessary. For example, destroying someone's brain is sufficient to bring about unconsciousness, but since there are other ways of bringing about unconsciousness, the destruction of someone's brain is not *necessary* to bring about that effect.

402. (E) Accordingly, the statement "If it rains, it will get wet" qualifies as a causal conditional. On the other hand, there are conditionals that are *not* causal. For example, here is a statement that is conditional but not causal: "If Shakespeare did not write *A Merchant in Venice*, then Francis Bacon did."

403. (A) For example, the statement "The rainstorm was the cause of the flood" would be interpreted, on such an analysis, as "If the rainstorm had not occurred, the flood would not have occurred."

404. (B) According to occasionalism, mental events do not interact causally with other mental events nor with physical events, and physical events do not interact causally with other physical events nor with mental events. Rather, all events are caused individually by special acts of a supernatural entity.

405. (E) The universalism view describes natural laws in terms of relations that hold between universals. The antirealist view maintains that laws of nature do not have a mind-independent existence. According to the laws-are-necessarily-true view, there exists no possible world in which the laws of nature do not hold. The antireductionist view claims that laws of nature neither supervene on—nor are reducible to—other facts and treats those laws as mind-independently real. All four of these views express metaphysical positions on the laws of nature. Quantum indeterminacy just says that determinism, on a certain interpretation of it, breaks down at the quantum level. Hence, the answer must be (E).

406. (C) According to antireductionism about natural laws, the laws of nature neither supervene on, nor are reducible to, other facts.

407. (B) An overly simplistic, but illustrative, example would be the following "argument" explaining how there came to be ice cubes in my freezer:

(i) Water freezes at or below 0 degrees Celsius.
(ii) My freezer cooled the water in the ice-cube tray to below 0 degrees Celsius. Therefore,
(iii) The water in the ice-cube tray froze into ice cubes.

408. (B) Quantum indeterminacy is popularly thought of as the notion that the strict determinism we seem to observe at the macro level breaks down at the quantum level.

409. (A) The main complaint about the universalism view has been that the supposed relation between universals has been so inadequately described as to have been left altogether mysterious.

410. (B) Kant believed that some sort of concept of cause and effect is a precondition for intelligible experience. Hence, we could not have *arrived* at the notion of causality *through* our experience. Rather, we must *bring* such a notion *to* our experience.

411. (C) *Supervenience* refers to the idea of certain facts depending on ("supervening on") other, more basic facts.

412. (C) A libertarian, like a compatibilist and unlike a hard determinist, believes that free will exists. Unlike a compatibilist, and like a hard determinist, however, a libertarian believes that if free will exists, then determinism is false.

413. (A) *Hard determinism* is distinct from *soft determinism* (also referred to as *compatibilism*) in that hard determinism denies the existence of free will.

414. (E) If acts of free will are to be understood as undetermined events, then *free* acts are just events without causal explanation. In other words, *free* acts would just be random events.

415. (B) Unlike libertarianism and hard determinism, compatibilism (or soft determinism) holds that the existence of free will is not contradicted by the fact of a wholly deterministic universe.

416. (C) According to the principle of alternate possibilities, an agent is morally responsible for an action only if he or she could have acted otherwise. Frankfurt counterexamples consist of thought experiments that seem to show that agents can be morally responsible for actions even if they could not have acted otherwise.

417. (D) On one plausible interpretation of determinism, an agent's action can never be different from what it actually was, since every event has a sufficient cause. Hence, one could argue that if determinism is true, and if the principle of alternate possibilities is true, then no one is morally responsible for his or her actions.

418. (A) A determinist could readily accept that things could have been different from how they in fact are. However, for a determinist this would simply mean that a different set of causes would have to have been in place prior to the different set of events to necessitate *those* events rather than the other ones.

419. (B) Causal determinism simply says that every event has a causally sufficient cause and that causal links between events occur in predictable, intelligible ways that are describable as natural laws.

420. (C) Quantum physics describes something called *quantum indeterminacy*. According to quantum indeterminacy, particles at the quantum level do not behave in ways describable by deterministic models.

421. (B) Causal determinism simply says that every event has a sufficient determining cause. This in itself does not tell us whether or not free will exists. That is, one could espouse determinism and deny that free will exists (as hard determinists do), or one could espouse determinism and accept that free will exists (as soft determinists do).

422. (E) Libertarianism disagrees with soft determinism and hard determinism in its rejection of determinism. Soft determinism disagrees with libertarianism and hard determinism in its rejection of the incompatibility of free will and determinism. Hard determinism disagrees with soft determinism and libertarianism in its rejection of the existence of free will.

423. (C) This could not possibly constitute a sensible criticism of hard determinism, since hard determinism is the view that for *every* event, including human actions, there exists a prior determining event.

424. (C) Other examples of second-order desires include *hoping that one's cravings for sweets stop, wishing that one liked vegetables,* and *wanting one's desires to be more consistent.* For those compatibilists who believe acting freely means acting consistently with one's desires, second-order desires pose an interesting problem: must actions also be consistent with one's second-order desires to be considered free?

425. (A) Intuitively, the notion that every event has a causal explanation (even if we don't always know what it is) makes a lot of sense. After all, it would be odd if things "just happened" for no reason at all. At the same time, it also makes intuitive sense to make a distinction between actions that we do voluntarily (actions that are the result of our free will) and those that are involuntary (actions that are done without, or against, our free will). If we want to account easily for *both* of those intuitions, as many presumably do, compatibilism—or soft determinism—clearly wins out over incompatibilist positions like libertarianism and hard determinism.

426. (B) Hume's position is also recognizable as a *compatibilist,* or *soft determinist,* view, since he does not deny that free will exists, nor that every event has a sufficient cause. Hume's requirement for free action is simply that an agent play an active role within the causal chain that leads up to the action.

427. (B) Leibniz's law is also referred to as the *identity of indiscernibles* principle. Another way of expressing the law is as follows: x and y are identical if and only if every property belonging to x also belongs to y, and every property belonging to y also belongs to x.

428. (C) Mereology, also describable as the study of parthood relations, has origins that can be traced to the Greek philosophers, played an important role in medieval philosophy, continued to develop throughout the period of modern philosophy, and still receives much attention today, especially in analytic philosophy.

429. (E) The "ship of Theseus" case concerns a ship whose parts are slowly replaced over the course of a sea voyage. When it gets to its destination, it no longer has any of the parts it had when it began its journey. The first question this scenario typically raises is, "Is the ship at the end of the journey the same ship as the one at the beginning of the journey?" and soon other interesting metaphysical questions crop up as well. Questions about *personal identity,* however, are about the identity of *people,* and not of inanimate objects like ships.

430. (D) To illustrate this notion, let us suppose it is true, as is sometimes claimed, that all the molecules that constitute a person's body at birth will have been replaced by the time he or she reaches adulthood. This means that the baby and the adult are not the same collection of molecules. But since it is just the development of a single person we are talking about here, the baby and the adult *are* the same *person*. So relative to molecular composition, the baby and the adult are not identical. But relative to person-hood, the baby and the adult are identical. That is how relative identity works.

431. (B) Two cats can be more or less identical. For example, two same-sized gray tabbies are *more* identical to one another than are a skinny white Siamese and a Rubenesque black Persian. This "more-or-less" kind of identity is referred to as *quantitative identity*. On the other hand, any cat you point to can be *completely* identical only with itself. This "complete" kind of identity is referred to as *qualitative identity*.

432. (B) If x and y are in a *symmetric* relation, then x stands in the same relation to y as y stands to x. If x is in *reflexive* relation, then x is related to itself. If x and y and z are in a *transitive* relation, then whenever x is related to y, and y is related to z, then x is related to z.

433. (E) According to the principle of substitutivity, co-referring terms can always be replaced by each other in any sentence in which they occur, without changing the truth value of the sentence. If that were correct, we should be able to replace "evening star" with "morning star" in the sentence quoted; doing so, we'd end up with "Sam believes the morning star is Venus, but he does not believe the morning star is Venus." Whereas we supposed the original sentence to be true, this sentence must be false, since it contradicts itself. This means that co-referring terms cannot just be used interchangeably without loss of truth, and so the principle of substitutivity is incorrect.

434. (D) An oft-used example of a rigid designator is "Benjamin Franklin" (ignoring the fact that other people share that name!). Since Benjamin Franklin might have had a different life from the one he in fact did have, we could say that there are many "possible worlds" containing Benjamin Franklin (in some worlds, he never invented bifocals; in other worlds, he became good friends with King George III; and in yet further worlds, he actually invented the cotton gin). Yet it would still be *Benjamin Franklin* in all these possible worlds, and so "Benjamin Franklin" refers to the same person in all possible worlds containing Benjamin Franklin.

435. (C) Something is *necessary* if it is the case in *all* possible worlds. Something is *possible* if it is the case in *some* possible worlds. Something is *impossible* if it is the case in *no* possible worlds.

436. (B) This view is most notably espoused by David Lewis. Although Lewis has several plausible arguments for the view, the usual reaction to modal realism is an "incredulous stare," as Lewis himself puts it.

437. (B) *De re* directly translates to "of (the) thing," and *de dicto* directly translates to "of the word." Suppose I said, "I want to meet the smartest man in America." This sentence has two interpretations. On one interpretation, I declared my desire to meet a specific person that I already had in mind, who just happens to be the smartest American. On the other interpretation, I simply declared my desire to meet the smartest man in America, *whoever that may be*. The former is the *de re* interpretation, and the latter is the *de dicto* interpretation.

438. (D) On most perdurantist views of personal identity, a person should be thought of as a four-dimensional whole with temporal parts. To make sense of this idea, imagine yourself at each moment of your life, from conception or birth all the way until death. At each of these moments, then, there is a "time-slice" of the person that is you. According to perdurance views, it is the whole collection of time-slices that constitutes the whole person, while each of the time-slices is just one part of the whole.

439. (B) According to mereological essentialism, a thing cannot lose or gain any parts without changing its identity. For example, suppose I have a ball of clay I call Plato. According to mereological essentialism, if I take some of the clay off the ball, Plato will no longer exist, since I now have a different ball (though I am free to call the new ball Plato as well!).

440. (E) Perhaps oversimplifying a bit: *A priori* truth is truth that can be ascertained apart from any specific experience. Necessary truth is something that is true in all possible worlds. Analytic truth is something that is true in virtue of meaning.

441. (B) A successful thought experiment in this case would show that two objects with all the same properties could be distinct, since that would violate Leibniz's law. The "two spheres" case does not meet this challenge for the simple fact that those objects do *not* have all the same properties.

Chapter 7: Epistemology

442. (C) Metaphysics is the study of the basic nature of reality and existence, and ontology is a branch of metaphysics specifically dedicated to questions about existence. Rationalism is an approach to philosophy that relies on reason and intuition to learn about reality, whereas empiricism is an approach to philosophy that relies on experience to learn about reality. Hence (A), (B), (D), and (E) are incorrect, leaving us with (C).

443. (C) Intuitively, if I did not believe something, I would not *know* it either. So knowledge requires belief. And if I *did* believe something, but it was false, then clearly I would not know it either. So knowledge requires truth. Finally, I might believe something, for no reason at all, that just happened to be true. Surely a luck guess does not count as knowledge! So knowledge also requires some sort of justification or evidence.

444. (A) Practical knowledge concerns "how-to" knowledge. For example, you might know *how to* ride a bike, or make a sandwich, or unify quantum mechanics and general relativity. Knowledge by acquaintance concerns knowledge as illustrated in the following examples: "She knows French," "He knows Hillary Clinton's dermatologist," "They know their way around a bottle of wine," "I know karate."

445. (D) I may have been certain that I would win, and I may have had conviction that I would win, but I still would not have *known* that I would win, so (A) and (B) cannot be correct. My belief *did* have content, namely, *that I will win*. So (C) is wrong. Since my belief was predictively successful, (E) is not right either. This means that my true belief did not rise to the level of knowledge because I lacked any *justification* for it (since I was just guessing).

446. (A) Perhaps the most famous example of a purported basic belief is René Descartes's claim "I think, therefore I am." According to Descartes, he could subject all his beliefs to methodological doubt, except for the belief in his own existence, since even if he doubted it, he would have to exist to do the doubting.

447. (B) Gettier cases consist of examples wherein an agent is justified in a true belief, but the truth of the belief is not connected correctly to the justification. For example, suppose I can always tell when my cat has come inside for the night by his empty food bowl, which I fill while he is away during the day. Today, like any day, I notice that his recently filled bowl is empty. I conclude that my cat has come inside for the night, which in fact *just happens* to be true. So by any ordinary standard of justification, my belief is justified, and it is also true. Unbeknownst to me, however, a neighbor's cat snuck in and ate all the food today, meaning that the empty food bowl did not actually signal my cat's retirement for the night. Many philosophers have the intuition that although I have a justified true belief in this case, I do not have knowledge.

448. (C) According to reliabilism, it is not sufficient for knowledge to simply have justification for a true belief—the belief must have been arrived at via a reliable, truth-tracking process. Reliabilism can therefore be seen as responding to the need created by Gettier cases to move beyond a simplistic "justified true belief" analysis of knowledge.

449. (B) According to internalism, in order to have knowledge one must have direct conscious access to everything that provides justification for a true belief. Externalism disagrees, claiming that we need not be explicitly aware of all the ins and outs of processes that reliably deliver the truth about the world.

450. (A) Coherentism, according to which a piece of knowledge should be thought of as a link in a well-ordered web of other links of knowledge, can be seen as a main rival to foundationalism, according to which a piece of knowledge should be thought of either as a foundational stone or as a stone resting on top of a solid foundation of basic beliefs.

451. (C) In the essay, Quine claims that since traditional philosophical attempts at analyzing knowledge have historically failed, philosophers should instead think of studying knowledge using more scientific methods of inquiry.

452. (A) For example, in the *Theaetetus*, Plato ends up defining knowledge as true belief "of which an account has been given." The *account giving* that Plato refers to can easily be seen as being more or less synonymous with *justification*.

453. (B) Externalism is the view that one need not always have conscious access to the actual basis of one's true belief in order to be justified in holding the belief. Reliabilism, in its simplest formulation, is the view that knowledge is true belief arrived at through a reliable process. Since reliabilism does not require that this process be directly accessible to the potential knower, it is least threatened by the claims of externalism.

454. (B) According to coherentism, a belief may be justified on the basis of how well it fits in with a coherent set of preexisting beliefs. The problem this poses if one adheres to a correspondence theory of truth is that a belief may not correspond to reality, and yet it may fit in perfectly with a consistent set of truths.

455. (C) Many philosophers have the intuition that such cases show that one can have a justified true belief without having knowledge. Contemporary analyses of knowledge are typically expected to include some attempt at dealing with this intuition.

456. (B) A counterpart to virtue epistemology exists in ethics: *virtue ethics*. Both of these theories emphasize the doer over the deed. That is, in virtue epistemology it is *knowers* that are primarily evaluated, not *knowledge claims*, and in virtue ethics it is *moral agents* that are primarily evaluated, not *moral acts*.

457. (D). (A), (B), (C), and (E) are all statements that can be known to be true *in virtue of the meaning of the words in the statement*, and being true (or false) in virtue of meaning is the identifying mark of any analytic statement. (D), on the other hand, cannot simply be known to be true by examining the meaning of the words, since it is a question of empirical fact whether Socrates will take an umbrella with him if he has one and it rains.

458. (E) Rationalism is an approach to philosophy that relies on reason and intuition to learn about reality, so (A) is incorrect. Epistemology is the study of the nature and scope of knowledge, and metaphysics is the study of the basic nature of reality and existence, which eliminates (B) and (C) as correct answers. Internalism, in the context of epistemology, is the view that the justificatory basis for a true belief is always accessible to the believer, so (D) is not correct. Having eliminated all but (E), we can conclude that the correct answer is *empiricism*, which is indeed an approach to philosophy that relies on experience to gain knowledge about reality.

459. (B) *A priori* statements stand in contrast with *a posteriori* statements. *A posteriori* statements are those whose truth value can only be determined by consulting experience, whereas *a priori* statements can be evaluated for truth simply by consulting reason or intuition.

460. (B) Plato is typically interpreted as claiming that everyday reality, as interpreted by the senses, is fleeting and ephemeral. True knowledge, on this view, concerns eternal truths that lie beyond the world of mere appearances.

461. (C) "It is time to go" expresses a full *proposition*, which means that it can refer only to an object of propositional knowledge: "I know *that* it is time to go."

462. (C) Synthetic truth is expressed in statements that are true not merely on account of meaning. *A priori* truth is expressed in statements that are known to be true apart from experience. Necessary truth is expressed in statements that are true in all possible worlds. *A posteriori* truth is expressed in statements that are known to be true via the senses. Hence, (A), (B), (D), and (E) must be incorrect, leaving us with (C) as the correct answer.

463. (E) For example, Descartes writes in his *Meditations on First Philosophy*, "I now seem to be able to lay it down as a general rule that whatever I perceive very clearly and distinctly is true."

464. (A) *A posteriori* knowledge is best contrasted with *a priori* knowledge, which is knowledge arrived at via reason and intuition alone, apart from experience.

465. (B) The philosopher most associated with idealism is George Berkeley. One of Berkeley's most famous dictums is *Esse est percipi*, which means "To be is to be perceived."

466. (C) Rationalists believe either that the senses do not deliver knowledge about reality at all, or that important truths may be arrived at simply by cogitation. Rationalism is traditionally associated with philosophers such as Plato, Descartes, Spinoza, Leibniz, and Kant.

467. (B) Mathematical truths are often held to be *analytic*, or true in virtue of meaning, although Kant held mathematical truths to be *synthetic*. This means that (A) and (D) are incorrect. Most philosophers also believe mathematical truth to be true apart from experience, as well as in all possible worlds, and so *necessary*, so (C) and (E) do not contain the correct answer either. This eliminates all answers but (B).

468. (A) According to Kant, space and time are categories that are *preconditions* of experience and therefore do not find their source *within* experience. Rather, our minds "organize" raw experience so as to make it spatially and temporally intelligible to us.

469. (A) Kripke points out that it was not always known that Hesperus and Phosphorus are both the same planet, but that it was discovered via empirical means. Kripke also argues that the identity between Hesperus and Phosphorus is necessary, so that there must exist necessary *a posteriori* truths after all.

470. (C) In the "allegory of the cave," Plato asks the reader to imagine a group of prisoners who have been chained to a wall inside of a dark cave their entire lives. These people are bound in such a way that they can only see the blank wall to which they are chained. Whenever objects pass in front of the fire behind them, the prisoners see dark shapes moving across the blank wall. Since this "shadow play" is the only thing the cave dwellers ever see, they believe it to be ultimate reality. Little do they know that what they think of as actual is merely a shadow of true reality. Plato draws an analogy between this scenario and the human condition: most of us mistake the sights and sounds around us for true reality. The philosopher, however, is like a person who has escaped the shadowy world of the cave and has seen the true face of reality under the full light of day.

471. (E) The claim that one cannot know the contents of another's mind is not one that is espoused by most philosophers. Rather, it is a problem to be solved. Perhaps the most well-known solution to the problem of other minds is the *argument from analogy*.

472. (A) Kant distinguished between two senses of *noumena*, a negative sense and a positive sense. According to the former, *noumena* simply refers to whatever lies beyond the realm of the senses. Kant believed noumena, according to that sense, do exist. According to the positive sense, noumena are objects not accessible to the senses, but accessible to pure reason or a mode of intuition wholly apart from the senses. Kant denied the existence or intelligibility of noumena in this sense.

473. (C) When confronted with the "dreaming argument" for the first time, people are often tempted to point to some telltale phenomenon by which they can usually tell that they are not dreaming. For example, when people are awake, they lack certain marvelous abilities they have when dreaming (such as flying). The reason that pointing to such distinguishing experiential features does not address the argument, however, is that it is entirely possible for a dream to completely mimic waking reality.

474. (C) The mere possibility that he is dreaming does not convince Descartes that he could be wrong about mathematical knowledge. To suspend judgment even about mathematics, Descartes imagines the possibility that an evil demon is actually twisting his mind to such an extent as to call into doubt his knowledge of basic mathematical truths.

475. (E) Here is an example illustrating the principle: "I know that I have a skeleton, and if I know that I have a skeleton, I know that I have bones. Therefore, I know that I have bones."

476. (D) According to the argument from analogy, I can conclude that other people have minds just as I have a mind because other people are sufficiently like me (they have brains, behave more or less like me, etc.) that such a conclusion is likely to be accurate.

477. (C) An empiricist is someone who believes that knowledge is primarily or exclusively arrived at via the senses. Purported *a priori* knowledge is knowledge supposedly arrived at through reason or intuition alone. Hence, an empiricist would be suspicious of *a priori* claims of knowledge.

478. (D) Moore intended this statement to offer proof that at least two things exist in the external world. Some have claimed that such a proof begs the question. Moore, however, believed that the claim that at least two things exist in the external world is as likely to be true as, or more likely to be true than, any of the premises used by skeptics.

479. (C) Methodological skepticism is for Descartes primarily a way of suspending judgment on all beliefs susceptible to any shred of doubt in order to provide a solid foundation for true knowledge. Descartes likened the process of methodological doubt to removing all the apples from a basket and putting back only those that are free of rot.

480. (E) For Hume, the truths of mathematics would have their basis in the "relations of ideas." As such, mathematical truths are demonstrable apart from any particular (and dubitable) experience.

481. (D) According to Putnam, the word *vat* would refer only to objects whose existence is causally related to your use of the word *vat*. Since your use of the word *vat* would be causally related only to something like *vat-images* (since you see only images as a brain in a vat), your word *vat* could not refer to the vat that your brain is actually in. So you would not be able to say, truthfully, "I am a brain in a vat."

482. (B) According to the closure principle, we know everything that is entailed by what we know. Some formulations of the closure principle also require that we know what is entailed by our knowledge in order to know the entailments.

483. (B) Methodological skepticism brackets knowledge temporarily, for a specific purpose. Academic skepticism asserts that we know nothing (or very little). Pyrrhonian skepticism makes no absolute claims about knowledge, but simply refuses to assent to any claim that is not evident.

484. (D) Although this scenario is sometimes a popular "stoner-philosopher" trope, most philosophers would dismiss the idea that a character in someone's dream could possibly have personal, subjective experiences, as being thinking subjects of personal experiences would entail their reality.

485. (A) The notion that knowledge is infallible is the notion that all alternate possibilities to a claim's truth must be disproved before the true belief can rightfully be accepted as knowledge.

486. (C) According to Descartes, in order to doubt anything, there must be a doubter. Hence, if I doubt anything at all, I must exist to do the doubting. This means that it might be possible for me to doubt the truth about anything, but I could never doubt my own existence as a doubter.

487. (C) According to Lewis, any skeptical possibility I am presently ignoring, I am *properly* ignoring. That is, so long as I do not attend to the skeptical alternatives to my justified true belief, I have knowledge. As soon as I attend to skeptical possibilities, however, my knowledge is "destroyed."

488. (C) Epistemic contextualism is a *semantic* theory about the word *know*. According to contextualism, the meaning contributed by the word *know* to the sentences in which it occurs can change depending on the context in which the sentence is uttered.

489. (D) *Semantics* in general has to do with the meaning of words and statements. Unlike traditional epistemological theories, which are concerned with *knowledge*, semantic theories of knowledge have to do with the meaning of the word *know* (and cognates).

490. (C) Contextualism also claims that the sense or meaning of the word *know* is not stable across all circumstances, but is liable to change according to the practical requirements of the context.

491. (A) Subject-sensitive invariantism agrees with epistemic contextualism that the "stakes" (how important it is to some relevant party that the knowledge claimed be accurate) affect whether or not the knowledge claim expresses a truth. They disagree, however, in how exactly stakes affect this outcome.

492. (A) One of the main ways of motivating epistemic contextualism is to argue that contextualism is the only way to explain certain linguistic intuitions. This criticism of contextualism alleges that those intuitions are better explained another way.

493. (C) According to some defenders of epistemic contextualism, the skeptic's standards are much higher than they normally are, and than they ordinarily need to be. This means that the skeptic is correct in the sense that knowledge, on the high skeptical standards, is impossible. But it also means that the skeptic is incorrect in the sense that ordinary knowledge claims are often true, on the lower standards appropriate for everyday situations.

494. (D) Contrastivism agrees with contextualism about the claim that sentences of the form "*s* knows that *p*" express different propositions in different contexts. According to contrastivism, however, this semantic variability is due to the "deep structure" of ordinary knowledge statements rather than to the semantic contribution of the word *know*.

495. (A) Another example, used by the cognitive scientist and linguist Steven Pinker, is "If you could pass the guacamole, that would be awesome." This statement *semantically* just states that the addressee's ability to pass the guacamole would be most impressive. Pragmatically, however, the speaker of that sentence is trying to convey that he or she would like the addressee to pass the guacamole.

496. (D) According to invariantism, the semantic contribution of the word *know* in statements in which it occurs does not change across statements. As such, invariantism directly denies the central thesis of epistemic contextualism.

497. (E) The relativist model of the semantics of *know* represents a relatively recent development in the semantics of knowledge. Given the current resurgence of interest in relativism, however, we can expect debates surrounding relativism and the semantics of knowledge to move to the forefront of contemporary epistemology.

498. (A) This claim is supported by the existence of linguistic intuitions that appear to be best explained by the thesis that it is the attributor of knowledge rather than the purported subject of knowledge that determines the level of the standard of justification.

499. **(C)** An indexical is an expression or term whose reference changes from context to context. The references of *here*, *I*, *tomorrow*, and *that* all change depending on who uses the words, and when or where the words are used. *Meaning*, however, does not depend in this extreme way on context to determine reference.

500. **(A)** The main motivation for epistemic contextualism consists of a set of intuitions that seem to show that the truth of knowledge claims and knowledge denials depends on highly contextual factors. This dependency is quite easily explained on the hypothesis that the semantic contribution of the word *know* to sentences in which it occurs depends on certain practical or pragmatic factors that are apt to change from context to context. The challenge for invariantism is to come up with an explanation that is equally natural and simple.